Arrow Rock

PROJECT SPONSORS

Missouri Center for the Book
Western Historical Manuscript Collection,
    University of Missouri–Columbia

SPECIAL THANKS

Christine Montgomery, Photographic Specialist,
    State Historical Society of Missouri, Columbia

John Viessman, Museum Curator,
    Missouri Department of Natural Resources

MISSOURI HERITAGE READERS
General Editor, Rebecca B. Schroeder

Each Missouri Heritage Reader explores a particular aspect of the state's rich cultural heritage. Focusing on people, places, historical events, and the details of daily life, these books illustrate the ways in which people from all parts of the world contributed to the development of the state and the region. The books incorporate documentary and oral history, folklore, and informal literature in a way that makes these resources accessible to all Missourians.

Intended primarily for adult new readers, these books will also be invaluable to readers of all ages interested in the cultural and social history of Missouri.

Other Books in the Series

Arrow Rock

The Story of a Missouri Village

Authorene Wilson Phillips

University of Missouri Press
Columbia

Copyright © 2005 by
The Curators of the University of Missouri
University of Missouri Press, Columbia, Missouri 65201
Printed and bound in the United States of America

Library of Congress Cataloging-in-Publication Data

Phillips, Authorene Wilson, 1938-
  Arrow Rock : the story of a Missouri village / Authorene Wilson Phillips.
      p. cm. — (Missouri heritage readers)
  Includes bibliographical references and index.
  ISBN 978-0-8262-1575-8 (alk. paper)
  1. Arrow Rock (Mo.)—History. I. Title. II. Series.
  F474.A77P48 2005
  977.8'47—dc22   2005002032

♾™ This paper meets the requirements of the
American National Standard for Permanence of Paper
for Printed Library Materials, Z39.48, 1984.

Typefaces: ITC New Baskerville and Lily Ann Shaded

This book is dedicated

To Ruth Wilson Banks Perry,
who shared her life history with me,
linking me to the past of Arrow Rock

And to my grandchildren,
Rachel Anne, Evan Charles,
Connor Alan, Caleb Alexander,
Elizabeth Grace, and
Carmen Authorene Elizabeth,
who link me to the future.

Contents

Acknowledgments

I am grateful to those historians and travelers who recorded early Arrow Rock history during their lifetimes, preserving Arrow Rock's past, and to those who, throughout the years, have maintained a village where this history can come alive for visitors. This book would not have been possible without their contributions and those of oral historians who shared their remembrances of village life during the last half of the twentieth century.

The Friends of Arrow Rock continue the work to preserve the village, and through the Friends I met Ruth Wilson Banks Perry, whose story inspired my interest in the history of the village. When Ruth died in 1997, she was buried in Sappington Cemetery with nearly three hundred and fifty black Missourians, including ancestors and relatives, who had called Arrow Rock home. Only fragmentary accounts of individual lives of those buried there survive, but visitors to Arrow Rock can see reminders of their work throughout the village.

I greatly appreciate the suggestions made by Rebecca Schroeder, general editor of the Missouri Heritage Readers series, and the editorial guidance of Sara Davis of the University of Missouri Press.

Arrow Rock

Introduction

Arrow Rock once meant a rock formation near a crossing on the Missouri River; these days, "Arrow Rock" means a small historic Missouri village. Throughout its history, it has most often been a place to pass through, or briefly visit, rather than a place to settle.

When Missouri's major thoroughfare west was the Missouri River, Arrow Rock was an important stop along the route. The town's leaders held enormous political power and wealth. Three Missouri governors called it home, and one of its early residents saved thousands of lives with his medical discoveries. The painter who came to be known as the "Missouri artist," George Caleb Bingham, helped found the village and built a home there. The Bingham house, along with much else that existed in nineteenth-century Arrow Rock, remains. The once-flourishing town was bypassed by the railroads and major roadways, and by the changes they brought.

Since the early twentieth century, villagers have welcomed visitors and travelers, but not everyone was welcomed during the early years. Native Americans, the area's first residents, often did not welcome the white trappers, who wanted their furs, or the settlers, who wanted their lands. Later, American pioneers did not welcome roving Indian bands, and the state soon forced Native Americans to go farther west. Some residents did not welcome the stream of Mormons moving west, in spite of the trade they brought. Saline County's militia eagerly helped drive Mormons from the state when the governor declared them enemies.

Others were forced to stay. Some early residents brought slaves with them, and from its earliest days, the area depended on slave labor for its economic prosperity. During the Civil War, residents were deeply divided on the issue of slavery, and soldiers from both sides were unwelcome intruders to some villagers. When African Americans were finally freed, they were segregated and often provided fewer services and educational opportunities than their neighbors. The last decades of the nineteenth century and the first of the twentieth brought hard times to the area, and many residents had to leave the village to survive.

Now a National Historic Site, Arrow Rock relives its long history in educational events, festivals, museum exhibits, and reenactments. In this book, some important moments in that history are offered in chronological order. Names of village settlers, visitors, and passersby enter and reenter the story. Details of the area's past give meaning to its present and to the times in American history Arrow Rock experienced—early days of settlement, an era of power and prosperity for some residents, incredible hardship for others, wars, a decline, and a rebirth. The long roll call of those who visited the area would provide a history of the opening of the West.

The ways in which the village has preserved its past illuminates for today's visitors, dependent on technology for their lifestyles, a time when modern luxuries and modern problems did not exist. Throughout the years, local historians and some descendants of the first settlers have tried to understand and interpret Arrow Rock's past. While its history is representative of that of other river towns, reminders of an earlier era are preserved in a village that continues to welcome the world.

Chapter 1

Pierre à Fleche
1673–1813

Native Americans were the first to know the area around the impressive rock formation above the wide river. French and Spanish explorers, soldiers, miners, and fur traders came later, and after the Louisiana Purchase, American explorers, soldiers, traders, and settlers learned of it. Thousands passed by. A few came to stay.

Long before there was an American village on the river now called Missouri, or a state by that name, there was an Indian trail beginning near the Mississippi River and leading westward to a place in present-day Saline County the French called *Pierre à fleche*, "rock of arrows." For centuries before European missionaries and explorers arrived, Indian tribes lived and hunted in the area. In 1673 explorers Jacques Marquette, a missionary, and Louis Jolliet, a trader, seeking a water route to the East Indies, came down the Mississippi River from Canada with Indian guides. Marquette drew a map that showed Osage Indian villages located two hundred miles to the west on the Osage River in present-day Missouri. He wrote of speaking to another tribe near the mouth of what is now the Missouri River. Marquette's name for these people, "ouemissourit," inscribed in Old French on his map, is the origin of the name by which we know the tribe, the river, and the state today.

The people who came to be called Missouris settled for a time at the mouth of the Grand River but eventually moved west to a "row of grassy hills now called the Pinnacles and built their village there."

Anthropologist Robert Bray wrote, "We may believe that the Missouri were happy there, and for many years they lived amid the beauties of nature, hunting buffalo and deer, fishing in the river and swamps, tending their crops and carrying on other activities . . . they became numerous, powerful, and perhaps rich by Indian standards of the day." The Missouri were great travelers, leaving their village not only to hunt, but to meet newcomers to the area and, later, to help their friends, the French. In 1712 they traveled to Detroit to help defend the post against the Fox. French adventurer Etienne Veniard de Bourgmont, "whose explorations provide the earliest detailed information about Missouri and its people," as his biographer wrote, returned to their village with them and made his headquarters there while he explored the area.

Bourgmont reported that the Missouri "are of very good blood." In 1714, with their help, he explored the Missouri River up to the Platte, describing the Indian tribes and the plant and animal life along the way. The same year a son he called "Petite Missouri" was born to Bourgmont and a daughter of a Missouri chief. When he returned to France a few years later, he took his son with him. In France, Bourgmont was declared "Commandant of the Missouri River," and a "Knight of the Order of St. Louis." He persuaded the French government to send him back for further exploration and to build a fort officials wanted to discourage Spanish expansion into the Missouri Valley. During the winter of 1723–1724, French soldiers under Bourgmont's command built the fort across the river from the Missouri village with the help of Indian women from nearby villages. Bourgmont named it Fort Orleans in honor of the Duke of Orleans, regent for young Louis XV.

Perhaps the French planned to promote mining on the Riviere de la Mine, as the Lamine River was called on early maps of the region. Bourgmont had reported that the Indians were taking lead from a nearby mine. Philippe Renault came to the Upper Louisiana Territory west of the Mississippi in the 1720s, bringing miners and slaves from San Domingo. He established mining operations near Ste. Genevieve, and historians speculate that he or some of his agents may have been responsible for the extensive lead mining that left traces a few miles south of Pierre à fleche and southwest toward the Lamine.

When Bourgmont returned to France in 1725, representatives of several Indian tribes, including the daughter of the head chief of the Missouris, accompanied him. The French welcomed the visitors, calling the young woman the "Missouri Princess." She married a French soldier at Notre Dame Cathedral. Historians do not know if she ever returned to her people on the Missouri. She was living across the Mississippi River from Ste. Genevieve, in Kaskaskia, in the Illinois country, in the 1750s when she showed a French traveler the watch the young French king had given her.

In 1764 when the teenage Auguste Chouteau and workers were building a trading post on the site that would become St. Louis, several hundred Missouri Indians arrived and told Chouteau they wanted to settle nearby. Chouteau sent for his stepfather, Pierre de Laclède, to negotiate with them, but meanwhile hired the women to dig the cellar for the trading post. According to historian William Foley, Laclède persuaded the Missouris they would be safer in their villages on the Missouri than at the isolated trading post.

By the late 1700s the Little Osage had established a village near the Missouri tribe to take part in the trade along the Missouri River. In *The Osage,* Willard Rollings reported that the tribe had separated into three bands by that time. While the Little Osage lived in their villages on the Missouri River, the group that became known as the Arkansas band had moved to the south along the lower Verdigris River, and the Big Osage remained along the upper Osage River, where they had been when Marquette drew his map. The Osage called themselves "children of the Middle Waters" and followed the tradition of moving from their villages to locate buffalo herds, then returning to harvest corn, squash, herbs, nuts, and berries. Most of the year was spent securing food for daily use and storing provisions for winter. Winter was a time for entertainment; like the Greeks, the Osage gathered around campfires to sing and tell stories. They valued hospitality; strangers received food, tobacco, and protection while in their company. The Osage were a religious people. Their elaborate rituals included daily prayers and baths. They had marriage and other ceremonies and worshiped a being they called "Wah Kon Dah."

The Indian Trail running west from the Mississippi led across the

☾   Native American tools. French explorers, the first Europeans in the area, named the flint rock outcropping from which Native Americans formed these arrowheads and scrapers "Pierre à fleche." The darker the stone, the more flint in the rock. Flint produces the spark when two stones are rubbed together, making it more valuable. A farmer in Saline County found these artifacts in his fields. (Courtesy Edgar A. Phillips)

Missouri at Pierre à fleche, which was later called "*the* Arrow Rock" or the "Big Arrow Rock" by Americans. There the great prairie plains and the forest met and merged. The rock rose ninety feet from the Missouri River. Its flint made ideal points for arrows. Since outcroppings of flint were rare, the Arrow Rock became a gathering place for arrowhead makers of many tribes. In addition, nearby salt springs attracted animals, which, in turn, drew Indian hunters, traders, and trappers. All needed meat as well as salt for preserving meat, seasoning food, and tanning leather.

Although Indian tribes often fought one another, the Indians and French lived in relative peace in Upper Louisiana for almost a hundred years. Game was plentiful. The French found a ready market in Europe for animal pelts, and the Indians enjoyed the goods—such as tobacco, brandy, scissors, and cloth—the French traded for the pelts. Spain owned the Louisiana Territory from 1762 to 1800, but for the most part it retained the French local officials in Upper Louisiana, then known as "Spanish Illinois." Spanish officials were not as successful in dealing with Native American tribes as the French. The Osage often raided villages along the Mississippi to get horses and supplies. A French military engineer traveling in Spanish Illinois in the 1790s wrote: "As swift afoot as a deer, which they track in the hunt, the Osages never spot a loose horse without feeling a passionate desire to steal it." The French negotiated to get their property back. The Spanish officials grew more and more impatient and encouraged other tribes to attack the Osage.

Trouble with the Indians, and British incursions from Canada, led the newly appointed Spanish governor in New Orleans, Baron de Carondelet, to issue a decree in 1792 opening the fur trade to all subjects of "His Catholic Majesty, the King of Spain." By the time France regained ownership of the territory in 1800, Americans, including Daniel Boone's family, had begun settling west of the Mississippi. In 1803 Emperor Napoleon of France sold the Louisiana Territory, almost 830,000 square miles, to the United States for about fifteen million dollars. By that time, most of the Missouri Indians, decimated by disease and war, had moved upriver to join the Oto tribe. Some joined the Osage. The Pottowatomie, Sauk, and Fox tribes were still located west of the Mississippi and north of the Missouri River. The Osage tribe dominated an area west of the Mississippi and south of the Missouri River to the Arkansas River in Kansas. These lands provided the diversity necessary for the Osage way of life—land to grow corn, woods to provide shelter and hunting grounds, and plains for hunting buffalo. Aside from Spanish explorers and French fur traders, few whites had ventured into the interior of Missouri before the Louisiana Purchase. When the territory was transferred to the United States, most Indians—even those who signed treaties with the new government—thought that they were simply allowing the newcomers to hunt on their lands. Individual ownership of land was not a practice most Native Americans accepted, but their lives were to change all too rapidly with the coming of the Americans.

In the spring of 1804, Meriwether Lewis and William Clark started on an expedition long planned by President Thomas Jefferson. Their mission was to explore the vast new lands west of the Mississippi, in the hope of finding a waterway to the Pacific Ocean. Leaders of the expedition arranged for a large keelboat and two light boats called *pirogues* to carry the provisions and the forty-five men, which included soldiers, Kentucky volunteers, French boatmen, and Clark's slave, York. Lewis's big black Newfoundland dog, Seaman, accompanied the "Corps of Discovery," as the explorers called themselves. They left St. Charles on the afternoon of May 23, 1804. On June 9 the expedition passed "the big arrow rock" and "the little arrow rock," as Clark noted. Lewis wrote in his journal that at a meadow called Prairie of the Arrows the Missouri River narrowed to two hundred yards. Moving upriver the keelboat twice caught on snags. The second time, the boat then swung around into a very dangerous position, broadside to the current. Some of the men swam ashore with a tow rope and soon got the boat to the safety of an island to camp.

The explorers reached the Pacific, although they failed to find a navigable route all the way to the ocean. On their return in 1806, Lewis, Clark, and others reported to President Jefferson the wonders they had seen on the long journey. The president, Clark, and others believed that there was land enough for both the increasing American population and the Native Americans, but the president wanted to remove the Indians farther westward, out of the path of the whites already moving into the new territory. The U.S. government planned posts and promised trade centers so that Indians could trade for supplies in exchange for the valuable furs they could provide. Officials hoped they would soon adopt European ways and settle down and farm, as some southeastern tribes had done.

Settlers were not far behind the explorers. After Daniel Boone's family had settled near St. Charles, Nathan, Daniel's youngest son, discovered a salt lick while hunting on Osage lands near the Missouri River. In 1805 he returned to the lick, two hundred miles up the

BOONES LICK SPRING, SONS OF DANIEL BOONE MAKING SALT.
1807

Boone's Saltworks. To produce salt, workers boiled water from the saline springs until only white crystals were left. The Boones placed the crystals in pirogues or hollowed sycamore logs, covered them with mud, and floated the salt downriver to St. Charles and St. Louis. Settlers used salt to flavor and preserve food and to tan and preserve animal skins. (Mural by Victor Higgins, Missouri state capitol, courtesy State Historical Society of Missouri, Columbia)

Missouri River, across from Pierre à fleche. Nathan and his brother Daniel Morgan Boone soon established a thriving salt-production business there and both the lick and the surrounding area came to be known as "Boone's Lick."

In August 1808, William Clark, then superintendent of Indian Affairs at St. Louis and brigadier general of the Territorial Militia, called upon Nathan Boone, an ensign in the militia, to serve as scout for the expedition to establish the trading post that the U.S. government had promised the Indians. Clark took eighty-one men, in six keelboats, from Fort Bellefontaine under the command of Captain Eli Clemson to build the fort. The group camped across the Missouri River from Pierre à fleche on August 31, 1808, where Clark recorded: "From St. Charles to this place Arrow Rock is 155 m[iles] estimated by land. [The] river is 200 yds wide." The next morning, using a dugout canoe, Clark crossed the Missouri River. At the foot of the bluffs he found an excellent rocky landing with a little valley beside it. He and his men walked up the valley to the top of the bluff, where they camped, prepared breakfast, and tended their guns before returning to their boats.

Clark's group continued to present-day Jackson County, where they established Fort Osage. On their return trip in mid-September, Clark noted that they "passed the Little arrow Rock at Sunset which is about 6 miles above the Big arrow rock by water and 2 1/2 or 3 [miles] by land. This Spot is handsome for a fort being only a point projecting with a high rich bottom below . . . river narrow and opposit bottom a mile wide, this is also a handsome Spot for a Town. We arrived after dark at the arrow rock where we crossed going out." The next day, Clark wrote, "We leave this Handsome Spot at 2 oClock . . . the situation is elegant Comdg [commanding] and helthy, the land about it fine well timbered and watered." As planned, sixty mounted riflemen joined Clark there for the return trip to St. Louis, and the word was soon out about this promising area of Missouri, so much like Kentucky, with plentiful game, trees, and fertile land.

The year the fort was built, 1808, Colonel Benjamin Cooper and his family moved near the Boones' saltworks. They built a cabin about a mile below Arrow Rock. Because the government recognized Osage Indian rights, however, Territorial Governor Meriwether Lewis ordered the Coopers to move out. They moved back downriver to Loutre Island, in the Missouri River below the mouth of the Gasconade, where Cooper's brothers Sarshall and Braxton joined them. All returned to the Boone's Lick area in 1810, taking their families with them. Nearly forty persons arrived in the area that spring. Benjamin Cooper continued to lead families to settle across the river from what some travelers now called the big Arrow Rock.

On April 2, 1811, writer Henry M. Brackenridge set off from St. Charles on a barge, "the best that ever ascended the river . . . manned with twenty stout oarsmen," armed with a "swivel on the bow and two brass blunderbusses in the cabin." He was traveling west with Manuel Lisa, "chief owner of the Missouri Fur Company. Mr. Lisa, who had been a sea captain, took great pains in rigging his boat with a good mast, and main and topsail, these being great help in navigation."

Lisa was trying to overtake an expedition sent by John Jacob Astor, founder of the American Fur Company, which had left a few weeks earlier.

Also on board, according to Brackenridge's *Journal of a Voyage up the River Missouri,* was "a Frenchman named Charboneau, with his wife, an Indian woman of the Snake Nation, both of whom had accompanied Lewis and Clark to the Pacific and were of great service." The interpreter Toussaint Charbonneau, his wife Sacajawea, and their infant son had joined the Lewis and Clark expedition during its stop at the Mandan villages. On the return trip they had remained at the village, although Clark had offered to take them to St. Louis. Soon after leaving the Mandans, Clark wrote Charbonneau, inviting him to bring Sacajawea and their son, Baptiste, "my danceing boy," to St. Louis. He offered to raise the boy and see to his education. Sometime in 1809 Charbonneau and Sacajawea had come downriver to St. Louis to put their son in Clark's care. St. Louis did not have a priest in residence, so a priest from Illinois baptized the child on December 28, 1809. Clark was in Washington at the time, and Lewis had died from a gunshot wound a few months earlier at an inn on the Natchez Trace. Auguste Chouteau signed the baptismal certificate as the child's godfather.

Some historians have contended that it was not Sacajawea on the boat with Charbonneau, but his other Shoshone wife, Otter Woman, believing that Sacajawea would have stayed in St. Louis with her son. Brackenridge, however, an American lawyer persuaded by Lisa to join the expedition as a hunter, was fluent in French. In the 1790s his father had sent him from Pittsburgh to Ste. Genevieve, when he was only seven years old, to learn French. He stayed and attended school with the French children. Although he does not mention Sacajawea by name, Brackenridge would have understood the French spoken by Charbonneau and would not have mistaken his wife's identity.

Sacajawea, who had been kidnapped from her people as a young girl, had indeed been of great service to Lewis and Clark. Brackenridge described her as "a good creature of a mild and gentle disposition, greatly attached to the whites, whose manners and dress she tries to imitate, but she had also become sickly and longed to revisit her native country." Most historians believe that Sacajawea died late the next year at Fort Manuel, which Lisa built about seventy miles south of present-day Bismarck, North Dakota. John C. Luttig, a St. Louis trader, and chief clerk at Fort Manuel, wrote on December 20, "a clear and moderate Sunday" that "This evening the wife of Charbonneau . . . died of a putrid fever." Although he did not give her name, he described her as about twenty-five, the age Sacajawea would have been. He added that she was "a good woman, the best in the fort." She left an infant girl, about four months old, named Lizette. After Fort Manuel was repeatedly attacked during the winter, Lisa took Lizette to St. Louis. In August 1813, Luttig asked the Orphan's Court of St. Louis to appoint him guardian of Charbonneau's children. Later, his employer, William Clark, became their guardian.

Brackenridge reported that the 1811 trip upriver was hazardous for Lisa's barge, with heavy rain, high winds, and obstacles, such as "fallen trees, sand bars, and drowned buffalos floating down river." However on Sunday, April 14, they came in sight of the Mine River, where there were "valuable salt works." The raft "put to shore at the farm of Braxton Cooper, a worthy man, who has the management of the salt works. The settlement is but one year old, but is already considerable and increasing rapidly; it consists of seventy-five families, the greater part living on the banks of the river in the space of four or five miles. They are generally persons in good circumstances, most of them have slaves."

Although settlers came up the Missouri River to the area, it was less costly to come overland. Many walked, drove carts, or rode horses from St. Louis over trails which generally ran north of the river, where the land was flatter, to the bluffs at the Arrow Rock crossing. Some historians believe that as early as 1811 a ferry was operating at that location. As more settlers arrived, roving bands of Indians pilfered and shot cattle in the settlements and at the saltworks. Probably because of these attacks, the Boones sold their salt operation in 1811 to James Morrison. However, settlers continued coming into the area, including brothers Samuel and William McMahan, David Jones, who had served in the Revolutionary War, and Steven Turley along with their families.

In 1812 when the U.S. declared war on England, Indians friendly to the English threatened the settlements. The Osage Indians had been generally friendly toward the newcomers, but the Sauk and Fox tribes were less so. Joseph Cooper, Sarshall Cooper's son, wrote: "The Indians were very friendly toward us, excepting they would occasionally steal our horses and put us to some trouble to recover them, until about March 1812, when they killed two of our men. The savages horribly mutilated their bodies and took their heads and hearts and placed them on poles." Officials urged settlers to move back east. This letter from area resident Sarshall Cooper to the territorial governor shows the pioneers' determination to defend their homes:

> We have maid our hoams here & all we hav is here & it wud ruen us to Leave now. We be all good Americans, not a Tory or one of his Pups among us, & we hav 2 hundred Men and Boys that will Fight to the last and we have 100 Wimen and Girls that will tak there places wh. makes a good force. So we can Defend this Settlement wh. with Gods help we will do. So if we had a fiew barls of Powder and 2 hundred Lead is all we ask.

The settlers prepared for war. Most cabins were built as parts of forts. The Coopers and those that joined them established Cooper's Fort, which was located about a mile and a half below the big Arrow Rock, across the river from the present-day village of Arrow Rock. Half a mile back from the river, in the river bottom between the timber and the river, Cooper's Fort was the largest of the five forts in the area. The twenty-one families and many young single men who lived there were always concerned about Indian uprisings, so they farmed the two hundred fifty acres as a common field instead of farming individual plots.

Baptist missionary John Mason Peck wrote that those who worked in the distant field "were divided into plowmen and sentinels."

> The one party followed the plows, and the other, with rifles loaded and ready, scouted around the field on every side. . . . Often the plowman walked over the field, guiding his horses . . . with his loaded rifle slung on his back. . . . When these detachments were in the cornfield, if the enemy threatened the fort, the sound of the horn gave the alarm, and all rushed to the rescue.

In 1813 Indians killed James and Samuel McMahan, beheading Samuel, near the Anderson-McMahan Fort. The settlements, far from the developed United States, were impossible for the U.S. Army to protect. Men of the area chose to organize. President James Madison appointed Nathan Boone the first leader of a ranger's group known as the Minutemen of the Frontier. Daniel Morgan Boone became a major, and Sarshall Cooper became a captain. Many men joined, and they patrolled all of the central Missouri Territory.

As a result of the war between the United States and England, as well as policies to resettle Indian tribes from the eastern United States, many Native Americans moved west as more white settlers, some bringing slaves, arrived from the east. Resident Indian tribes continued hostilities to discourage this influx of white settlers and emigrating eastern tribes. The army closed Fort Osage, forcing George Sibley, whose assignment had been to trade with and counsel the Indians, to leave. He planned a similar facility near the Arrow Rock in order to fulfill the government's obligation to continue trading with the Osage. The 1808 treaty negotiated by William Clark, later amended by Meriwether Lewis, had promised the Osage supplies and a place to trade as well as blacksmithing and other services in exchange for a large part of their lands.

On August 28, 1813, Sibley began purchasing goods to trade and weapons to defend the trading post that he planned to build. He set off from St. Louis up the Mississippi River on September 24, continuing up the Missouri River to the Arrow Rock site. Sibley chose the spot that Clark had suggested, at the top of the bluff above the Big Arrow Rock, approximately one mile north of the present-day town, for the new post. According to his end-of-the-year inventory, the post was a two-story blockhouse, thirty feet by twenty, "built of cottonwood logs, roofed with oak slabs well secured by spiked-on hickory splits, and armed with one swivel gun and three blunderbusses." Sibley reported that the post provided plenty of room for trade goods and weapons. A line of double log huts housed Sibley, his servant, the interpreter, Antoine Burda, and five hired men. Sibley was ready for the winter as well as for trade.

On Sunday morning, November 28, 1813, the Little Osage leader, called Big Soldier by the Americans, was among those who came to

Sibley's Post, Arrow Rock (1813–1814), was a two-story building, twenty by thirty feet, built of cottonwood logs. A stockade of logs protected the trading post and other buildings. George Sibley believed the trading posts established by the U.S government helped the Indians by providing supplies they needed in exchange for their furs. (Drawing by Kate L. Gregg from original specifications, courtesy State Historical Society of Missouri, Columbia)

Sibley Post to meet with Sibley. Although he answered to the American's name for him, Big Soldier and other Little Osage men preferred being referred to as "little" in deference to the one they considered "big," Wah Kon Dah. The white men were impressed with Big Soldier and the Osage, for most were over six feet tall, towering over the whites and other Indians. Adding to their imposing appearance was their roached hairstyle extending into a braid down the middle of the back. The rest of the head and face was smooth. Big Soldier wore bone earrings, and necklaces of bone and shells were hidden under his warm buffalo robe. His leggings and moccasins were made from deerskin.

The life Big Soldier's people had known was disappearing. They were being crowded out by the white settlers and Indian tribes forced from their eastern homelands. White hunters were depleting the game necessary for Osage survival. Diseases brought by the whites were wiping out entire villages. Many members of the tribe had already moved west. Although Indians now had horses and guns to hunt and metal tools and knives to make their work easier, they needed the supplies that the post at Arrow Rock offered. And so they had come to meet with Sibley, the agent of President Madison, who would pay the annuities promised in the Treaty of 1808.

Sibley, as he wrote, "endeavored by all means within my power to attain the wishes of the Osage." Interpreters had taken down the words of the Indian leaders as they discussed the closing of Fort Osage and the opening of the Arrow Rock post. In his work on the early history of the area, Richard Forry brought together some of the speeches made by the Indians, which William D. Lay has published in "Indian Trade Factories and Forts in the Boonslick, 1812–1815."

The Big Osage for the most part welcomed the move. The head warrior of the Big Osage declared that his people did not like Fort Osage, which they called Fort Clark, "for very good reasons. The road between that place and our place is . . . a very dangerous one to travel. Our enemies lay in wait for us. . . . I think we will be more secure coming here because of the large settlement of Americans near this place." He also thought it was better "on account of our being able to procure provisions here from the Settlers when we need any."

The Little Osage opposed the new place and wanted the post at

Fort Osage reopened. Big Soldier, who had been on missions to Washington twice, spoke angrily:

> Whose fault is it that these two villages are divided? The "Big Red Head" [Clark] built a fort at the Fire Prairie—Old White Hair as well as my chief agreed to settle there. We have kept our promises, they have not remembered theirs. . . . The Trading House is not for nothing. We have given our sons for it and I tell you plainly that I think the President has done very wrong to remove it at all. I have seen him and his Country and millions of his people and am very certain that he is able to protect a Trading House wherever he is bound by Contact to keep one. I do not like this place at all.

Also attending the meeting at the post was trapper Ezekiel Williams, who had been captured by the Kansas Indians in June 1813, while on his way down the Arkansas River from the Rocky Mountains. The Indians had released him in August but kept all his furs. Williams wrote authorities in St. Louis, who notified Sibley. When Williams learned that the Indians were going to receive their supplies, he came to the post to make a claim for his lost furs. Sibley informed the Kansas Indians that since Williams was a citizen of the government for which he (Sibley) was acting, he would not give them their supplies unless they returned the furs. At first they denied having Williams's furs, but finally they went to their lodges and returned with packages that bore the initials "E. W." They brought bundles until they were only one bundle short; Williams agreed to this settlement.

On this November day in 1813, Big Soldier listened while Sibley negotiated peace between Ezekiel Williams and the Kansas. He listened as Sibley urged the Indians to settle in territory to the west, which was to become Kansas and Oklahoma, build permanent houses, and farm.

Big Soldier listened, but he was not completely persuaded. As he told Sibley later:

> I see and admire your manner of living, your good warm houses, your extensive fields of corn, your gardens, your cows, oxen, workhouses, wagons, and a thousand machines, that I know not

🄰   Some historians believe this drawing of an Osage Warrior by French artist Charles Balthazar Saint-Memin, c. 1805–1807, is a likeness of Big Soldier, who visited Washington, D.C., twice after the Louisiana Purchase. (Collection of New-York Historical Society)

the use of. I see that you are able to clothe yourselves, even from weeds and grass. In short you can do almost what you choose. You whites possess the power of subduing almost every animal to your use. You are surrounded by slaves. Everything about you is in chains, and you are slaves yourselves. I fear if I should exchange my pursuits for yours, I too should become a slave. Talk to my sons, perhaps they may be persuaded to adopt your fashions . . . but for myself I was born free, was raised free, and wish to die free.

Sibley confessed, in a letter reporting Big Soldier's words to Thomas L. McKenney in 1820, "I was in vain to combat this good man's opinion with argument." The Little Osage leader knew change was coming. It was not something he wanted. As he told Sibley: "I am perfectly content with my condition."

The day after the meeting with the Osage, William Sherley Williams left from Arrow Rock with dispatches from Sibley for General Clark in St. Louis. Williams, later to be known throughout the west as "Old Bill," was not to become the best of the mountain men, according to one historian, but he was one of the most interesting. His exploits were legendary. The Williams family had come to the St. Louis area before the Louisiana Purchase, and Bill had grown up near St. Charles during the Spanish Colonial period. He first became a preacher, then took up hunting and scouting, and by 1813 was living with the Osage. The Osage would soon be leaving their traditional villages, and men like Bill Williams would explore and open the West. The trickle of settlers would become a stream and then a flood. Still, most only passed by the Arrow Rock and headed on westward.

Chapter 2

The Arrow Rock
1814–1820

William Clark, whose journal of the 1804–1806 "Voyage of Discovery" had referred to "the cliff called the Arrow Rock," drew a map in 1814, noting the Boonslick area near the middle of the Missouri Territory, stretching along the Missouri River and its major tributaries. Included on it was the area now known as Chariton, Cooper, Howard, and Saline counties, where "*the* Arrow Rock" was located. In his journal, Clark referred to the area as "Boons lick," and the country was variously known as Boone's Lick, Boonslick, or Boon's Lick. However the name was spelled, the area continued to attract settlers from the east, especially the southeast, in spite of increasing Indian resistance. Many of the newcomers brought slaves.

County government and statehood would soon become issues for settlers, but first the remaining Native Americans had to be persuaded to move farther west to make room for the Americans. By 1794, according to Jean Baptiste Truteau, a schoolteacher in St. Louis who had become a trader, attacks by Mississippi tribes had driven the Little Osage from their village on the Missouri River. Several times they had taken refuge with the Big Osage at the Place-of-Many-Swans, which the French called *Marais des Cygnes*. This time they stayed. They had found it too dangerous to be near the Missouri River after the Missouri tribe moved west.

Warring Sauk and Fox on the Mississippi came to visit the peaceful Sauk and Fox at their winter quarters on the Little Moniteau,

 *Cooper's Emigrant Train,* a mural by Victor Higgins in the Missouri state capitol, commemorates the early settlement of the Boonslick. (State Historical Society of Missouri, Columbia)

only forty miles from the Arrow Rock. Once largely peaceful toward Americans, some Osage began to join the more hostile tribes in attacking settlers. The growing population intensified the problems for the Native Americans. The buffalo, an essential source of food and clothing, were being killed in great numbers for their hides. George Sibley closed the post at the Arrow Rock in March 1814 as a result of the Indian uprisings, which had killed several settlers in isolated attacks, including two who had helped Sibley build his trading post.

In 1814 one of Cooper's group, Jesse Cox, crossed to the south side of the Missouri River about three miles above Arrow Rock, where he cleared land and "built a cabin of unhewn logs, a single story home about sixteen feet square." Cox and his son-in-law William Gregg and their families moved to the cabin, and soon the surrounding land was known as Cox's Bottom. Troubles with the Indians became constant. While taking care of chores, Gregg was ambushed and killed, and his daughter Patsy was captured. According to one account she was on a horse behind an Indian, with one hand tied to him. She grabbed his knife, cut the binding, and jumped to the ground.

Neighbors who had been pursuing the Indian rescued her as her captor fled.

The same year, Indians burned Anderson-McMahan Fort and broke up the saltworks. Braxton Cooper was killed while sawing logs for a new home, and Sarshall Cooper of Cooper's Fort was shot while sitting in his cabin holding his small daughter. John Mason Peck recorded what he had heard of the tragedy, still mourned in the community several years later. It had happened on a dark night. "Captain Cooper's residence formed one of the angles of the fort. A single brave crept stealthily in the darkness and storm to the logs of the cabin, and made an opening in the clay barely sufficient to admit the muzzle of his gun." The sentinel did not see him, and the shot he fired fatally wounded Cooper but left his daughter uninjured.

George Sibley wanted to reopen Fort Osage after the end of the war, but the law establishing government trading houses had expired in 1814. Despite some controversy about the usefulness of trading posts in winning the friendship of the Indians, Congress finally passed a new law in May 1815, and Sibley prepared to return to Fort Osage. He believed strongly in the factory system, which was intended to help the Indians by providing them with reasonably priced goods in return for their furs. Like Bourgmont, he had lived easily among Native Americans, accepting their differences and learning from them.

Osage historian John Joseph Mathews noted, "The [U.S.] government was fortunate to have men like Sibley and Clark as its representatives. . . . The Little Ones were fortunate to have them as liaisons with European civilization." Sibley and a few others, he wrote, seemed to be dedicated to justice and fair play. Mathews included William Sherley Williams among the "men of conscience and humanity sent to the Osage." Williams's biographer, Alpheus H. Favour, wrote that he went to the Osage as a missionary and was converted by them. As American missionaries of the time understood the Osage beliefs:

> They worshipped the sun because it gave light, warmth, and fertility; the moon, because it ruled the propagation of the Indians and animals; the earth because it nourished and supported them; and thunder because it was the source of rain. . . . It is said

that [Williams] offered to trade with them; that if they would accept the Christian religion he would become an Osage, and to this the chiefs and headmen agreed. Williams entered whole-heartedly into their life, and trapped, hunted, lived, and . . . associated in every way as an Indian among fellow Indians, [but] the Osage still revered the sun, moon, earth, and thunder as all-powerful spirits.

About 1813 Williams married a young Osage woman according to the customs of the tribe and lived with her in the Big Osage town on the Marais des Cygnes. The couple had two daughters in the next few years. Although the children were named Mary and Sarah, for his older sister and his mother, he participated in Osage life completely, gaining a "perfect speaking knowledge of the language" and serving as interpreter for George Sibley at Fort Osage.

Before leaving St. Louis to reestablish Fort Osage, Sibley had married fifteen-year-old Mary Easton, daughter of the first postmaster of St. Louis, Rufus Easton. According to biographical accounts of her life held at Lindenwood College, which George and Mary Sibley later founded, her wedding trip was by keelboat up the Missouri River from St. Louis. For her comfort in the home that Sibley had established at Fort Osage, Mary took her furniture, saddle horse, her library, and her piano with fife and drum attachments. Shortly after their arrival, Sibley wrote to his brother that "my wife seems much pleased and quite content. . . . She amuses me and herself every day for an hour or so with her piano on which she performs extremely well. . . . You may be sure that Mary is a very great favorite with the Indians. Indeed they literally idolize her since they have seen her play." When Mary's younger sister visited her at Fort Osage, Mary began classes for her and the young Indian girls who came to the fort.

In the fall of 1815 William Hayes and James Wilhite and their families arrived at Cooper's Fort across the river from the Arrow Rock. According to Napton, "The women walked and carried their babies in their arms, and assisted in driving the stock during the day when on the route, and upon camping at night built the fire and prepared the evening meal." After looking over the area across the river in the southern part of the big bottom, William Hayes took the first wagon—

reportedly "rather a 'shackly affair'"—into what is now Saline County.

Later that fall, Wilhite, Hayes, and others went upriver in canoes, found large bee trees, and brought back fifty-eight gallons of pure, strained honey. It was well known to the pioneers that bees came west with, or just ahead of, the Americans. As David McKinley wrote in "The White Man's Fly on the Frontier," in the July 1964 *Missouri Historical Review,* many travelers in the eastern states had observed that Native Americans called the bee the "Englishman's Fly." In 1750 bees were not yet found west of the Alleghenies. The English botanist John Bradbury wrote that they had first appeared in St. Louis in 1795. According to Bradbury, a French lady in St. Louis had received a jar of honey from Kaskaskia, and sent a young slave with a box to bring back two of the "flies" that made it. In 1804 Lewis and Clark found bees as far west as the mouth of the Kansas River.

Thomas Jefferson had observed in 1781 that to the Indians the bee was a sign of the white man's coming, and a Cass County resident reported that he had once witnessed Osage holding a mourning ceremony because a swarm of bees had been seen. To the whites, honey was a welcome treat on the frontier, and Timothy Flint wrote that by 1828 bees were growing scarce in the Boonslick country. Only eight years earlier Franklin resident August Storrs had gathered two hundred gallons of honey within a few days.

During the next years, more and more Americans were on the move; Indian troubles occurred less frequently, and settlers came to the Missouri Territory from eastern states; many from earlier settlements near St. Louis moved farther west. Former soldiers were looking for a new start, and farmland in the East was scarce. John Mason Peck reported: "Some families came in the spring, summer, and autumn of 1815; but in the winter, spring, summer, and autumn of 1816 they came like an avalanche. It seemed as though Kentucky and Tennessee were breaking up and moving to the 'Far West.' Caravan after caravan passed over the prairies of Illinois . . . all bound to Boone's Lick." A St. Charles resident agreed: "The whole current of immigration set towards the Boon's Lick country. . . . Boon's Lick was the common center of hopes, and the common point of union for the people. Ask one of them whither he was moving, and the answer was, 'To Boon's Lick, to be sure.'"

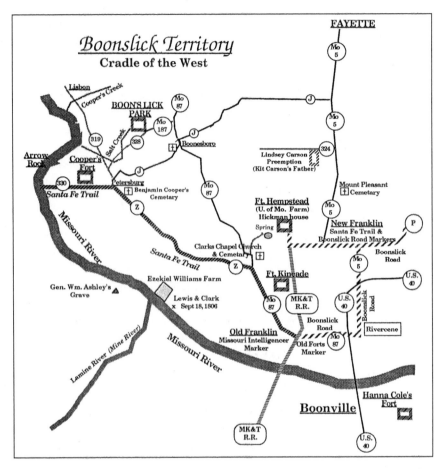

⊙   This map shows the westernmost settlements in the Boonslick in the first decades of the nineteenth century. By 1820 the population of the Boonslick area had reached 21,000. (Courtesy William D. Lay)

From Tennessee, where folks pronounced Arrow as "Airy," came Henry Nave and his wife, a sister to Daniel Thornton, who had arrived the year before and settled in what was known as Cox's Bottom. The Naves traveled in a wagon, but because the road was so poorly marked, they lost their way and nearly ran out of food, finally arriving at Cooper's Fort early in December. A few days later Mrs. Nave had a baby. On Christmas Day Mr. Nave crossed the river to present-day Saline County.

T. C. Rainy, later a resident of Arrow Rock, wrote this account after listening to Henry Nave himself:

> Henry secured two canoes, lashed them together, uncoupled his wagon, took the hind wheels and axle over at one trip, the fore wheels and tongue at another; then in successive trips, he ferried over the wagon bed and its contents. He selected a location for his cabin, cut down round poles for the walls, the rafters and joists for his frame-work, split out boards from a large tree for his roof, and puncheons for his floor. He found some large, flat stones, out of which he built his fire-place and hearth. The chimney was built of wood and the stones were placed inside as a lining. About the time he had his house covered and the chimney erected, the weather turned very cold. The freezing weather made it impossible for him to make up in the open the "mud mortar," used for the purpose of "chinking" the walls to keep out the cold, and of lining the chimney inside and outside with mud, as was necessary. He therefore built a fire in the middle of the cabin, by which means he thawed the earth underneath the fire. Then he dug up the earth near his fire and made his mortar inside.

Nave had brought apple and peach seeds and kept them through the winter in a large gourd near the fireplace. In the spring, he planted the first orchard in what was to become Saline County. Later Nave and Daniel Thornton sowed about three pecks of wheat—also a first.

Some of the new immigrants to the area were tradesmen who developed towns to provide services for settlers. Howard County was formed in 1816, and the town of Franklin was established the same year.

On January 1, 1817, the first of several men whose land in the southeastern part of the Missouri Territory was flooded or had been ruined for agriculture by the New Madrid earthquakes of 1811–1812 filed a claim in the Arrow Rock area. Land in what would be Saline County was claimed by several former residents of New Madrid when the U.S. government granted settlers affected by the earthquake other lands equal in amount to those lost. Some New Madrid claims were sold to speculators, leading to problems in the area. In 1814 Congress had passed the "Preemptive Act," which gave settlers who had "squatted" on public land before it was available for purchase the right to buy it before others who might want it, but preemptive rights did not extend to the areas in the western Boonslick that had been Indian Territory in 1814. It was not until January of 1819 that preemption rights were extended to Howard County. As soon as public land sales got under way in the land office in Franklin "bidding was feverish and prices were high," according to newspaper accounts. Whereas improved land in the St. Louis area sold for four to twelve dollars an acre, William Foley reports that "one particularly good section near Franklin brought over twenty-six dollars an acre."

The river crossing at the Arrow Rock served many of the newcomers. Judiah Osman received a license to operate a ferry in 1817, and historians believe that he was a ferryman at that crossing. By 1818, John Ferrill was operating both the tavern, which he built at the crossing, and the ferry, which had been constructed by putting a platform atop two dugout canoes and adding a railing to keep animals from falling off. On December 28, 1818, Reverend Nicholas Patterson wrote to a friend in St. Louis from the "Boon's Lick." His letter, published in the March 2001 *Boonslick Heritage,* provides a thoughtful and detailed view of pioneers and "newcomers" living near Arrow Rock. They were "real frontier people, a stalwart, uncultivated, rough race, always moving to the 'range,' beyond the influence of schools [and] the Gospel ministry. . . . Very few . . . can read, yet they have vigorous minds, and that species of enterprise that pushes them beyond the region of farms, houses, bridges and law."

Some planned to "remove to a more distant region," where they could find "plenty of deer, bear, and probably buffalo." Others intended to stay, establish farms, and build homes. Besides giving the history of the "persons of no small consequence" (among them Colonel Benjamin Cooper) who had first come to the region and settled, Patterson described others he met and observed in the Boonslick. The "uniform" for the "softer sex" was " a gown of coarse cotton, usually called "factory cloth" or "gingham," and covered with very narrow stripes or sometimes checks.

> The head gear is a bonnet of the same stuff, in the form that in
> the old States is called a sunbonnet. This is worn through the

day, in the house or out of it, especially when company is present. New customs, in many things, are singular. Very rarely will the wife and mother sit at the table with her husband. At least this is invariably the case when strangers are present. Many of the females are modest, tidy, and industrious. All perform domestic labor, even when they have servants. I have found but few exceptions.

Patterson ran across a local preacher in the woods who wore a "hunting shirt, so called."

A kind of loose, open frock, with large sleeves, the body open in front, lapped over and belted with a leather girdle and buckle. The cape, or shoulder piece, was large and fringed. Its material was dressed deer skin, of yellowish cast. His vest and pants were made of cloth, a mixture of wool and cotton, of light blue color. He wore leggings of dressed skin and a pair of moccasins in place of boots. He carried a rifle on his shoulder, . . . and a large knife stuck in his belt. For a covering to the head he wore a sort of cap made of wolf's skin, with the hair on, and the tail fastened up behind.

Stuart Voss quotes *Emigrants Directory of 1817,* which reports that the Boonslick was "probably the easiest part of the world to . . . farm in." The settler had "only to locate himself on the edge of the prairie, and he has the one half of his farm a heavy forest and the other half a fertile plain or meadow, he has then only to fence in his ground and put in his crop." One early settler, however, remembered the hardships: "During the summer all travel had to be at night and pioneer fields plowed at night because of the green-head fly." Nevertheless, new settlers kept arriving. As Sibley wrote in 1817: "Swarms of immigrants are daily arriving here from Virginia, Tennessee, and Kentucky, and among them are several gentleman of very considerable wealth."

A party from Stephen H. Long's government expedition to Yellowstone boarded the Arrow Rock ferry on July 19, 1819. Edwin James, botanist and geologist to the expedition, using the observations of Long and others, noted that from the summit of Arrow Rock there was a pleasing view of the river. He described the ferry, "the earliest west of Franklin," with its railing, as "one particularly adapted to the navigation of a rapid stream." That was fortunate, as "Near the base [of the Arrow Rock] is a remarkable eddy, which as they were crossing, whirled their ferry boat entirely around."

The hunting party found game scarce. "Most of the deer, and larger animals, as well as turkies, have fled from this part of the country, though it is but a few years since they were extremely abundant." After leaving the river bottom the expedition party saw only raccoon and some other small animals and birds. The land, however, was promising. Passing some small scattered oak trees and bushes, they arrived at the margin of a wide grassy plain, which spread before them "as varied and apparently as boundless as the ocean."

James had estimated that on the "prolific and inexhaustible soil" of the river bottom, the labor of one slave was "sufficient for the culture of twenty acres of Indian corn and produces ordinarily about sixty bushels per acre, at a single crop." In Kentucky "in the most fertile parts, the products of agriculture [are] about one third less than in the best lands on the Missouri."

Supplies and many people continued to arrive by canoe, keelboat, and raft. The first steamboat to make its way up the river was the *Independence,* commanded by Captain Nelson. Leaving St. Louis on May 15, 1819, the *Independence* arrived in the Boonslick country on May 28. It went on to the Chariton River and then returned to St. Louis with goods picked up in ports along the way. The *Western Engineer,* part of an expedition sent out by Congress, caused considerable attention the next month when it steamed up the Missouri disguised as a sea serpent, in an attempt to intimidate hostile Indians. It failed in its mission to reach the Yellowstone River, stopped not by hostile Indians but by hazards of the river. The new steamboats offered faster travel on the Missouri River, but they were dangerous. Their boilers could build up too much steam and explode. Probably worse, the meandering Missouri River bed was clogged with trees and sand, which steamboats had trouble avoiding. Many steamboats sank, resulting in great loss of life and property.

As early as 1806 President Jefferson had signed a bill to build a national road from Maryland to St. Louis; meanwhile, travelers

⟲ Titian Peale's painting of the *Western Engineer* shows its most famous feature, the exhaust system. When it was disguised to look like a huge water serpent in the hope of discouraging hostile Indians, "the vessel seemed to be carried on a monster of the deep, smoking . . . and lashing the waves." It never reached its destination, the Yellowstone River; the Missouri proved too much for it. (American Philosophical Society)

going west from St. Louis generally followed winding, unmarked Indian trails. Early settlers also took what they called the Boonslick Trail, used by the Boones to transport the iron kettles for their salt-production endeavor; it began at St. Charles and ran north of the Missouri River, passing seven miles south of present-day Fulton and Columbia to Old Franklin, similar to the route of Old U.S. Highway 40. Settlers along the way worked to improve the common trails, to create roads, and Captain John R. Bell, the official journalist for the Long expedition, reported that the main road from St. Charles to Franklin was passable for carriages and wagons. In 1819 Ezekiel Williams and his neighbors laid out roads in the Boonslick area, including one from Cooper's Fort to the ferry at Arrow Rock.

An economic depression in 1819 and worn-out soil in the South led farmers from Virginia, Tennessee, and Kentucky to migrate to the fertile Boonslick area and try to establish new hemp and tobacco plantations. Plantations required large numbers of workers, and they had to be largely self-sufficient in isolated areas. Those who could brought slaves to work the land. John Sappington, who would become one of the most famous of the new settlers, moved to the newly formed Howard County in 1817. Born in Maryland in 1776, he moved with his family to Nashville, Tennessee, at nine. He studied medicine in Nashville under his father, and probably while practicing for a year in Kentucky, he met Jane Breathitt, whose brother had served as a Kentucky governor. They were married in 1804, when Sappington was twenty-eight. Although he practiced medicine in Tennessee, he also started a business shipping cotton and tobacco to New Orleans and trading land and slaves.

Sappington's close friend Thomas Hardeman had moved to the Boonslick area and written back about the rich Missouri soil, high crop yields, and the successes of his sons, John and Baily, as well as his sons-in-law, George Burnet and Glen Owen, who had followed him. Sappington's interest was piqued, and when one of his neighbors, lawyer Thomas Hart Benton, moved to Missouri Territory and encouraged Sappington to follow, he moved with his family and settled near the future Arrow Rock. Meanwhile, Hardeman and his son John Locke had bought adjoining farms and lived for years in the same house five miles upstream from Franklin, then the westernmost town in Missouri. Their neighbor was former trapper Ezekiel Williams.

Families continued to arrive in the area. Joseph and Benjamin Huston were born in Philadelphia, Pennsylvania, but after their father died, their mother moved her five children back to her home in Virginia. Joseph married Sarah Brownlee in 1805, and in 1819 Joseph and Sarah, along with Benjamin and his family, and the Huston's uncle Joseph Burk and his family came to Missouri and settled a few miles from Arrow Rock.

The area had all the characteristics of the frontier. It offered endless opportunity, but danger was never far away. Historian Dick

Steward, writing of the first duel in western Missouri, in *Duels and the Roots of Violence in Missouri,* suggests that in the Boonslick area there existed "an atmosphere . . . where serious bodily harm and even death lurked just below the surface of civility." He writes:

> The first of the "western" duels in Missouri occurred in the Boonslick region in 1820. The Boonslick was the fastest-growing area in Missouri and a place where etiquette and formality were in short supply. In the spring of that year a highly spirited young military officer, Major Richard Gentry, rode swiftly out of the town of Franklin to overtake Henry Carroll, the twenty-eight-year-old son of Howard County's land registrar. Within minutes a pistol, or pistols, depending upon which account one wanted to believe, flashed, and young Carroll fell from his horse, mortally wounded. . . . The improvised killing, termed a duel by Gentry supporters and a murder by the Carroll faction, stemmed from long-standing factional jealousies, land claim disputes, and disagreements over politics and slavery. . . . It depicts the twin aspects of vengeance and justice on the Missouri frontier.

But progress continued. The Hardemans worked together to improve their farms, and John developed an agricultural showplace that he called Fruitage Farm. The family became prosperous producers of hemp, Missouri's first important cash crop. Hemp was a fibrous plant used to make a rough cloth, but more important, it was used to make rope, which was necessary to the marketing of the cotton crop in the South. John established "Hardeman's Garden," which became well known to travelers. Charles van Ravenswaay wrote that Hardeman's Garden, "famed as perhaps the first garden and plant experiment station in the Mississippi Valley. . . consisted of ten acres formally planned with a center maze, ornamental beds, pools, and 'shell-lined' paths." The Hardemans did "experimental breeding, seeding, and cultivation, and kept extensive records." They operated a nursery and supplied fruit trees, grapevine cuttings, and ornamental shrubs and trees for central Missouri, St. Louis, and Tennessee.

The Hardeman farm was on the trail approaching the crossing at Arrow Rock, used by nearly everyone traveling overland to the west.

Nicholas Perkins Hardeman, in *Wilderness Calling*, wrote: "The prominent location of the garden, directly on what soon became the principal artery of travel to the FartherWest and Far West, with its own steamboat landing and ferry boat facilities connecting with Arrow Rock and the Santa Fe Trail, contributed to its recognition as did the welcome extended by its creator." Many early visitors stopped by the Hardeman's and received a ready welcome. St. Louis's Henry Shaw, who later founded the Missouri Botanical Garden, visited Fruitage Farm as its fame grew. Thomas Hardeman opened a tavern near the river, and he and John operated a ferry service just south of Arrow Rock connecting Howard and Cooper counties.

Hardeman's friends, the Sappingtons, purchased thousands of acres in what would soon become Saline County. They built a two-story log structure five miles southwest of the Arrow Rock ferry crossing, in the area that was to become known as Sappington Settlement, naming the house and farm "Pilot Hickory." In addition to developing a large farming operation, Sappington continued his medical practice. A major health concern at this time was malaria, known as "ague" or "chills," which affected many settlers; 2 to 10 percent of those who contracted malaria died as a result. Many others were left with anemia and severe and prolonged weakness. The usual treatment for fever was giving a tonic after purging and bleeding the patient. Sappington did not believe in treating ailments by bleeding and purging; he and other doctors experimented with the bark of the cinchona tree from Peru, from which quinine was extracted. Sappington experimented with the strength and timing of the quinine doses, determining that it was best to begin the medication when symptoms of malaria first appeared, and his treatments were successful—people survived and were spared the weakness and anemia.

In 1820 the area sent its first exports east. Henry Nave, James Sappington, and John Hartgrove made canoes, loaded them with bacon, and floated downriver to St. Louis. They sold the bacon, then disposed of their boats, and returned home by land. In *Along the Old Trail*, Rainy related how Nave, wishing to raise hogs, had traded his wife's sidesaddle for two "shoats." He built a lot but soon turned the hogs out each day to feed on the abundant supply of acorns that fell from the oak trees, supplementing the corn used as feed. Rainy explained: "Feed was thus abundant and cheap, but the prowling wolves gave him [Nave] great anxiety by their incursions at night, when they made frequent attempts to carry off young pigs. The pioneer and his trusty dogs were often called out to repel a night attack."

In *The Genesis of Missouri,* Foley states that while fewer than 1,000 persons had lived in the area between the mouth of the Osage and the western Indian boundary in 1816, by 1820 the population was "in excess of 20,000, including 3,000 Afro-American slaves." Franklin, about twelve miles downriver from the Arrow Rock and the largest town in the interior of the Missouri Territory, "had 120 log houses by 1819, several of brick, and some two-story frame dwellings," according to Hardeman in *Wilderness Calling.* "Businesses and public buildings included thirteen general stores, two blacksmith shops, mills, taverns, billiard parlors, post office, printing press, court house, and a two-story jail. The population of about 1,000 included a number of people who, along with settlers in the nearby . . . area would loom prominent in the New West and in the state."

Local governments were a necessity. The districts established by the Spanish along the Mississippi had served as counties in Upper Louisiana for ten years. In 1812 Congress had established the Missouri Territory. When Howard County was formed from what had formerly been Indian lands in 1816, it encompassed what is now Chariton, Cooper, and Saline counties. Cooper separated from Howard in 1819, and in 1820 Saline was divided from Cooper County and named for its numerous salty springs and streams.

Establishing a state proved more difficult. Slavery became an important issue. By 1820, nearly one-sixth of the territory's population were slaves, and the percentage was higher in the Boonslick area. Even settlers who could not afford a slave generally agreed that people had a right to own slaves. However, Missouri lay north of the line that separated free states from slave states, and Congress was intent on keeping the number of slave states and free states equal. There was opposition to making Missouri a state, but finally, when Maine wanted to enter the Union as a free state, Missouri was allowed to enter as a slave state in an agreement known as the Missouri Compromise.

Chapter 3

A Stop on the Santa Fe Trail
1821–1828

As Thomas Shackelford noted in an address to the Missouri Historical Society in 1901, "It is well known that Missouri entered the union amid a great contest." The contest, as he said, was over "African slavery," and only after a bitter struggle had Congress arrived at the "Missouri Compromise," admitting Maine as a free state in 1820 and Missouri as a slave state in 1821. Shackelford was a native of Saline County, and much of his "Early Recollections of Missouri" was based on his life there.

When Missouri became the twenty-fourth state, "Arrow Rock" was still only the location of a rock formation on the Missouri River. Most travelers still arrived by boat, although some came overland. Saline County's new government chose as its first task laying out a road from Arrow Rock west through Grand Pass to Sibley, where George Sibley had reopened Fort Osage in 1815.

When word reached the Boonslick that Mexico had declared independence from Spain, residents of the area realized that Mexicans would need a new source of goods. Since the Panic of 1819 had left many Americans without funds to buy land and goods, William Becknell and others of the Boonslick saw the opportunity to solve their financial problems by developing a trade route overland to Santa Fe. Becknell, who had managed the Boone saltworks, worked as a ferryman, and served with Daniel Morgan Boone's Mounted Rangers in the Black Hawk War, led the first successful trading expedition to Santa Fe.

☉ Wagon and mule trains started west along this trail from the Big Spring through Arrow Rock. (Photo by author)

In June 1821, Becknell placed a notice in the *Missouri Intelligencer,* outlining a plan to organize a company of men to go westward for the purpose of trading. The notice assured readers, "No man shall receive more than another for his services, unless he furnishes more." All interested persons were to sign up by August 4, and a meeting would then take place at the home of Ezekiel Williams. On September 1, Becknell and several other men on horseback left with pack-horses loaded with goods and crossed the river "near the Arrow Rock ferry." The group stopped at the spring up the hill from the Arrow Rock crossing, which would become a watering stop for caravans headed to Santa Fe, and camped for the night six miles from the ferry. The route he took was to become known as the Santa Fe Trail, and Becknell became known as the "Father of the Santa Fe Trail."

Alphonso Wetmore wrote some years later,

> The enterprize was, at the time, deemed one of infinate peril;
> and the . . . venture was accordingly limited in amount; . . . the
> articles of merchandise . . . were suited either to Mexican or
> Indian taste. In the event of failure to reach the point of desti-
> nation, it was a part of the plan of the adventurous party to
> remunerate themselves with the capture of wild horses, or, in
> the manly . . . sport of the buffalo chase.

It was not until some weeks after leaving Arrow Rock that Becknell learned through a French interpreter traveling with Mexican soldiers that the Mexican Revolution had succeeded. The Santa Fe authorities welcomed the early traders, and when Becknell returned home in January 1822, he announced fabulous profits, mostly in gold and silver. In his account of the trip, published in the *Missouri Intelligencer,* he wrote, "The trade is very profitable; money and mules are plentiful, and they do not hesitate to pay the price demanded for an article which suits their purpose or their fancy." Becknell and others began to prepare for more trips to Santa Fe, and in the spring of 1822 Captain Benjamin Cooper led a caravan of twenty-one men, including his nephews Braxton and Stephen. They took three wagonloads of goods and returned in the fall with four hundred head of livestock, jacks, jennets, and mules and furs. For Becknell's second trip in 1822, he hired twenty-one men and loaded three wagons instead of pack mules. This trip was so successful that a woman who had invested sixty dollars in the venture received nine hundred dollars upon his return.

Another profitable trade was launched when the former lieutenant governor of the territory, William Ashley, opened what historian Robert Utley called the "generation of the Rocky Mountain trapper." Ashley's venture was to bring fame to such legendary mountain men as Jim Bridger and Jedediah Smith, as well as to Ashley himself, who had come from Virginia to Missouri before the Louisiana Purchase. Keelboats and steamboats were named in his honor, and "Ashley Beaver" came to signify extra-fine fur. Ashley and his partner, Andrew Henry, introduced the "annual rendezvous" to replace the trading-post system and recruited adventurous young men to live in the west and trap beaver.

To prepare for his venture, Ashley placed an ad "To Enterprising Young Men" in the *Missouri Republican* in St. Louis in 1832:

> The subscriber wishes to engage one hundred young men to ascend the Missouri River to its source, there to be employed for one, two, or three years. For particulars apply to Major Andrew Henry, near the lead mines in the County of Washington, who will ascend with and command the party, or of the subscriber near St. Louis.
>
> William H. Ashley

William Foley believes Major Henry was responsible for the three innovations that brought fame and, eventually, fortune to the company: an emphasis on trapping, rather than trading; the decision not to maintain a fortified trading post; and having the trappers operating as individual businessmen, not company employees. However, it was Ashley who gained the fame and fortune, including a poem in John Neihardt's epic cycle "Ashley's Hundred." Major Henry, who went "upriver at the head of Ashley's band," and spent almost two years in the mountains, withdrew from the company before it turned a profit. He had intended to go back but never did, according to Foley.

The "most adventurous of all the mountain men," according to Michael Patrick, signed on for one of Ashley's early trips. African American James Beckwith, later known as Jim Beckwourth, was to become one of the most famed of the mountain men of his time, but would be largely forgotten for many years afterward. Beckwith was born in Virginia, the son of slave owner Jennings Beckwith and a slave mother. Sometime before 1809, historian William Foley wrote, his father settled "in the isolated backwoods of the St. Charles district"; perhaps, Foley suggests, so as to give his biracial children better opportunities.

In 1824 Beckwith signed on as a member of Ashley's trapping expedition. Before his departure, his father went to court in St. Louis and signed a deed making his son's emancipation legal. He left St. Louis with Ashley as a free man. His autobiography, in which his name was changed, *The Life and Adventurers of James P. Beckwourth: Mountaineer, Scout, and Pioneer, and Chief of the Crow Nations of Indians,* was first published in 1856. Although many historians later discredited Beckwourth's claims, Patrick reports that more recent investigators have found that most of his experiences can be documented.

Ashley, who traveled up and down the Missouri River from 1822 until 1826, when he sold his Rocky Mountain Fur Company to William Sublette, must have found the Arrow Rock area appealing. In the 1830s he bought Chouteau Springs for $1.25 an acre, and when he died in 1838, he was buried, as he had requested, "on the crest of a bluff high above the Missouri River," not far from Arrow Rock. It was said he wanted to be buried where he could see the boats land at both Boonville and Arrow Rock. As for Jim Beckwourth, he became a trapper, Indian fighter, and scout, once rescuing Ashley from drowning. He lived with the Crow Nation, who considered him a long-lost member of the tribe, but after fourteen years, he returned to St. Louis. His family had moved from the area, and finding St. Louis much changed, he went to Florida to work for the U.S. Army for a time. Returning to St. Louis, he took a job with Andrew Sublette to trade with Indians in the Southwest, and set out along the Santa Fe Trail in 1838, the year of Ashley's death. After many adventures, he rejoined the Crow Indians at the request of U.S. officials. He died about 1866.

Expeditions to Santa Fe continued, and early trips, while hugely profitable, were not trouble-free. Some traders lost goods to Indian raids, and many of the men who made the trip suffered from malaria. Others contracted the disease on the trail. Malaria occurred during the summer months, striking people who lived or traveled along streams and creeks. Adjusting to the higher altitude along parts of the trail was especially difficult for those who were already sick. But an 1824 expedition was remarkable for its success. The 25 wagons, 80 men, and 150 horses were led by Stephen Cooper, accompanied by August Storrs and future governor Meredith Miles Marmaduke, who reported that the men were generally healthy. According to a biography of Sappington, the credit belonged at

THOMAS H. BENTON SPEAKING AT HIS DESK.

☉ Missouri Senator Thomas Hart Benton actively promoted westward expansion and frequently requested information about the Santa Fe trade. (State Historical Society of Missouri, Columbia)

least in part to the fact that Marmaduke's first stop on his journey was to obtain quinine, which was later given to any members of the expedition who even developed a headache. Marmaduke kept a journal of his trip, and Senator Thomas Hart Benton, realizing the economic promise of the new trade route, sent a questionnaire requesting details from Storrs, which he presented to the U.S. Senate on January 5, 1825.

Meanwhile, Arrow Rock was becoming better known to the nation and the world. Whether traveling on the Missouri River or over the trail, *the* Arrow Rock was on the route for all westward travelers— including those visiting from other countries. During his first tour of the continent, Paul Wilhelm, Duke of Wuerttemberg, was delayed seven miles south of the Arrow Rock when his cart broke down. In his memoirs, *Travels in North America, 1822–1824,* he reported that during the two hours it took to make necessary repairs, "countless blood-thirsty mosquitoes stung me. They seemed to like the interior of the forest even better than the region close to the river bank." The duke was not pleased with his fourteen-year-old driver nor with the "wretched hut" of the ferry owner. Although he conceded the family "were good hearted people," he complained, "We could get nothing at all to eat except some old milk which had almost turned to cheese and some dried-out cornbread." His rum had been left at an earlier stop, and he was fearful of drinking the water, explaining, "In this great heat, drinking water unmixed with some kind of spirituous drink is very harmful and may produce fever." But in spite of his problems, Duke Paul then recorded a remarkable description of the place, which he referred to as *Pierre de la Fleche:*

> The bank forming the *Pierre de la Fleche* is high and composed of beautiful rocks. This chain of hills on the right bank of the Missouri is hardly twelve English miles long and it gradually runs over to the lowland which extends as far as Franklin. . . . Nothing remarkable occurred during my crossing of the river on a raft. Requiring almost an entire hour to get across, the raft had to be pulled half an English mile up the stream. The current in the neighborhood of the rocks called *Pierre de la Fleche* is extremely swift and it was most difficult to make the raft fast on

the right bank. We climbed a rather high, steep hill on which nut trees and sassafras grew. On the ridge of these hills the timber becomes thinner. Forest and prairie alternate with one another. The vegetation becomes more luxuriant, the dense underbrush gives way to grass-covered spaces, and more and more the region takes on a lighter aspect clearly indicating the transition from the forest region to the prairie.

Although Paul Wilhelm enjoyed the sight of the prairie at first, he later concluded, "It appears picturesquely beautiful when it present[s] itself to the eye for the first time, but loses much of its interest, for its monotony wearies the senses."

At a trading post at the mouth of the Kansas River, Duke Paul met the young man that William Clark called "Pomp," Jean Baptiste Charbonneau, the son of Sacajawea and Toussaint Charbonneau. Clark, who had overseen Pomp's education, had told Duke Paul about him in St. Louis. In 1823, at age eighteen, he was working at the post for the Chouteau family. Paul later met Pomp's father at Council Bluffs, and Toussaint Charbonneau served as his guide for the rest of his trip west. On his return trip, Paul reached the Chouteau post in October, and on October 29, 1823, Pomp joined him for an eventful trip down the Missouri and the Mississippi rivers and across the Atlantic. Pomp spent the next seven years in Europe, living in Wuerttemberg and traveling with Paul.

In 1825 Congress designated the old Indian trail that passed from east to west near the Arrow Rock crossing a federal road, and the Osage signed another treaty, giving up title to their homelands in western Missouri; they moved their villages on the Osage to a territory in Kansas that the government had set aside for them. In the same year the U.S. government appointed three commissioners, including George Sibley, still living near Fort Osage, to survey and mark the route from the Missouri frontier to the New Mexico border. Among the scouts hired for the survey was Bill Williams. He had served as an interpreter at a trading post Sibley established at Marais des Cygnes and at Harmony Mission, but his wife had died in the early 1820s, and his Osage family and friends were leaving their village. He was ready to go west.

Although most travelers still went on beyond the Arrow Rock, some stayed, and their farms soon dotted the landscape. In 1826 floodwaters covered all the Missouri River bottom. Franklin was washed away. Most of its inhabitants relocated to higher ground, but some moved on west. One young saddler's apprentice who was destined to win fame as a trapper and a scout joined his older brothers on a wagon train headed to Santa Fe. Kit Carson had been two years old in 1811 when his family moved to the Boonslick and settled in Cooper's Bottom. While his father, Lindsey, was clearing a field, a fire broke out in a nearby woods. As Lindsey tried to extinguish the flames, a burning limb fell on him, killing him instantly. Kit's widowed mother persuaded her son to become an apprentice to Franklin saddlemaker David Workman. The apprenticeship did not work out, and on October 12, 1826, Workman placed a notice in the *Missouri Intelligencer:* "Christopher Carson, a boy about 16 years old, small of his age, but thick set, light hair, ran away from the subscriber to whom he had been bound to learn the saddler's trade. . . . All persons are notified not to harbor . . . or assist said boy under penalty of the law. One cent reward will be given to any person who will bring back the boy."

Carson's three older brothers had set out on the Santa Fe Trail, and he, "[b]y some means unknown . . . laid his hands on a mule and reached Independence just as his brothers were leaving." Kit's first trip along the trail was a "lesson in frontier survival," according to a biographer, but he learned to enjoy scouting and hunting on the way.

In May 1827, Ezekiel Williams, then living in Howard County, and about sixty men crossed the Missouri River on the ferry to the rocky beach below the big Arrow Rock and climbed the quarter-mile-long slope to Big Spring. Wagons loaded with goods were waiting. Additional wagons waited near the present border between Missouri and Kansas. The train grew to fifty-three wagons, the largest expedition yet to Santa Fe. Williams, commander of guards, was chosen captain for this trip. As he reached the spring at Arrow Rock, he might have looked to the north, where Sibley's trading post had stood, and recalled a meeting fourteen years earlier, when George Sibley, the government agent, had negotiated Williams's dispute with Kansas Indians over his furs.

At that meeting, Big Soldier had spoken angrily about the closing of Fort Osage by the government. Although it had reopened at the old location in 1815, it was now abandoned. Most of the Little Osage had relocated. In 1825 the state of Missouri had made it illegal to trade with Indians. Fewer Indians were in the area as Williams's expedition began the trip to Santa Fe, but there were also fewer animals, and like Williams, most trappers had turned to trading.

In June 1827 Big Soldier took part in an adventure he would remember for the rest of his life. He was one of six Osage, two women and four men, who left St. Louis for a journey to France in a plan developed by promoters, including French-born David Delauney. Some Americans who followed their adventures, including Thomas L. McKenney of the U.S. Office of Indian Affairs, believed that the Osage thought Delauney was taking them to Washington. Later historians believe that the Osage, unhappy with the Americans, wanted to see their French friends again.

The Osage visitors were welcomed warmly and entertained lavishly in France, as Bourgmont's group had been a century earlier, but it soon became clear that Delauney intended to make money from the "wild Indians." Thousands of French paid to see them, but eventually Delauney was jailed for an old debt and the Osage were left to wander around Europe, often penniless. One of the young women, Mohongo, gave birth to twins in Belgium, but only one child survived. Part of the group, including Mohongo and Big Soldier, finally reached Paris, and the Marquis de Lafayette, hearing of their plight, helped raise funds to send them home. They returned to their villages in the summer of 1830.

Several travelers reported seeing Big Soldier after the trip to France, always wearing the medal that Lafayette had given him. The painter John Mix Stanley saw him in Tahlequah, Oklahoma, in 1843 at an intertribal conference. Writing in his catalog of Indian paintings, later published by the Smithsonian Institution, Stanley reported that Big Soldier was "about seventy years of age, vigorous and active. . . . He wore a medal La Fayette had given him, which he prizes above everything on earth . . . and participated in all the various dances and amusements with as much zest as any of the young warriors."

 Saline County was formed from Cooper County just before Missouri entered the Union as a slave state. (State Historical Society of Missouri, Columbia)

The Osage were later to accept some of the ways of the Americans, as the "Five Civilized Tribes" had done, but in 1843 they were holding, as Big Soldier had predicted they would, to the old ways. According to Stanley, "They cultivate some corn but depend heavily upon the chase for subsistence, and repel all attempts toward civilization. . . . The introduction of missionary or civilized arts among them, has but little weight with them." They also still practiced their "passion for stealing, which they gratify on every occasion." Stanley thought that "like the Spartans, they deem it one of the attributes of a great man to pilfer from his neighbor or friend and avoid detection." He observed that if given something to keep, the Osage would defend it with their lives and return it when asked, "but the next instant will steal it, if they can do so without being detected." Big Soldier spent a week the following September with Stanley. He died the next year.

Ezekiel Williams and the men who returned in November 1827 from Santa Fe generated profits of around 40 percent, bringing back to Missouri eight hundred head of horses and mules worth twenty-eight thousand dollars. Local traders who made several trips from the Franklin area to Santa Fe while continuing to improve and develop their farms included William Becknell, Ezekiel Williams, William and Darwin Sappington, Meredith Miles Marmaduke, and James Smith, the son of General Thomas A. Smith, a Virginian, who came to Missouri after the War of 1812 and became one of the first to enter a land claim in Saline County. In 1827, a "gentleman from Saline county" wrote a friend that times were good. "Mules and asses are numerous since our intercourse with the Spaniards; they generally sell at 20 to 30 dollars. Beef cattle are sold at one dollar the hundred weight, on foot. Great numbers are driven to different parts; some go [to] the state of Ohio, and from there perhaps to Philadelphia and New York."

Marmaduke had married Lavinia Sappington, John Sappington's daughter, and moved to Saline County, where he and his brother-in-law Darwin Sappington started a store at Jonesboro (now Napton). Often wagons headed for Santa Fe were loaded there. The Santa Fe Trail departure point was moving farther west, but the crossing at Arrow Rock remained a hub of activity. Transporting supplies from the landings on the Missouri River to the developing center of the state was a big business. Sappington and Marmaduke built a warehouse and a brick store, probably near where the ferry landed. The store and the warehouse were ready to receive goods by steamboats, which were becoming safer. Goods were then delivered by wagon to customers in southern Saline County and even into Pettis County. From the warehouses they shipped hemp, tobacco, and hogs, produced by slaves on farms in the area, to eastern markets and to New Orleans.

Henry Vest Bingham, father of the future "Missouri artist," George Caleb Bingham, had come west from Virginia in 1818, searching for a place to relocate his family. The following year he settled in Howard County, where he operated a popular tavern-hotel north of the public square in Franklin, and according to William Foley, "quickly won acceptance in the booming community." Henry bought a farm not far from his brother John's near Arrow Rock, where he began cultivating tobacco and established a facility for processing it while continuing to work and live in Franklin.

When Henry Bingham died in 1823, his wife, Mary, moved the family to the Saline County farm, where she opened a school to support herself and the seven children. Except for George, her sons went to work for area farmers. Since George was not interested in farming, he served as a janitor for his mother's school and in 1828 apprenticed to a Boonville cabinetmaker and Methodist minister, Justinian Williams. He continued to sketch pictures, a practice he had started while still in Virginia, according to biographer Paul Nagel, drawing on fence posts and sides of barns.

Even with increasing numbers of settlers in the area, no village had yet been laid out near the big Arrow Rock on the Missouri River. Many of the settlers had come from the South, and they generally followed the tradition in which landowners did not live in town but encouraged merchants and businessmen to settle there to provide needed services and build churches and schools. Slaveholders, of course, meant to establish plantations like those they had left behind and produce crops to sell to local and eastern markets, but interest in establishing a town near the Missouri River was growing, and in the next decade the site was to become known to an increasing number of traders, settlers, and travelers. By 1830 Saline County would have a population of 2,146, including 706 slaves, and the new town would soon draw businesses and churches.

Chapter 4

New Philadelphia
Becomes Arrow Rock
1829–1844

E arly arrivals to the Boonslick area had first settled along the waterways. As a consequence, floods took a heavy toll on pioneers like John Hardeman, whose Hardeman Gardens on his well-known Fruitage Farm was lost to the Missouri River. In an effort to recoup his losses through trade, Hardeman took to the Santa Fe Trail in the late 1820s. On the return trip, he contracted yellow fever and died, leaving his second wife and their small children, Glen and Leon. Hardeman's older son, John Locke, who was single, remained on Fruitage Farm, although floods continued to wash away the property.

Interested citizens, among them Henry Nave, Thomas A. Smith, and several Binghams, including eighteen-year-old George, met on May 23, 1829, to discuss organizing a town near the Arrow Rock, high above the flood waters. They chose commissioners to select a site from several that were offered by landowners. In the end, Burton and Nancy Lawless and John and Mary Bingham each deeded twenty-five acres of land for the new venture. In addition, Lawless allowed the town the use of the springs on his land, known to Santa Fe Trail travelers as "Big Spring," located on the eastern edge of the proposed town.

Marmaduke, who had been judge of Saline County, now served as surveyor of the county. In 1829 he platted a town, which he called

"Philadelphia," perhaps because he used a plan similar to that of Philadelphia, Pennsylvania, or perhaps because local merchants generally traded in that eastern city. The town was sometimes called New Philadelphia. A notice from the *Fayette Intelligencer* of July 3, 1829, listed the proposed town's attributes.

Town of Philadelphia

THIS TOWN is situated in SALINE COUNTY, on the Missouri river, about twelve miles above Franklin, at a point known by the name of Arrow Rock. It is laid out on a high bluff, and commands a handsome view of the River, and has several excellent Springs adjoining. This point, as a place of business, possesses as great natural advantages as any other, having around it an extensive country of the best farming land in the State, with a good and rapidly increasing population of wealthy and enterprising citizens, which never fail of furnishing large quantities of surplus produce and articles for exportation, which forms a considerable part of our commerce. The main road from St. Louis to Liberty crosses at this point, and roads in every direction from this place will always be dry and good.

Title indisputed, the land being purchased from the United States.

LOTS

Will be offered for sale on the premises to the highest bidder, on the 24th of July next. A credit of twelve months will be allowed to purchasers, by their giving bond with approved security.

For the encouragement of those who wish to vest their funds in town property, the proceeds arising from the sale of lots are to be applied to the improvement of the Town.

Among the "wealthy and enterprising" citizens making an impact in the area were the ones who were listed as the commissioners desiring to sell lots in the newly formed town: Joseph Patterson, a carpenter, who lived in a log cabin near the Arrow Rock crossing on the Missouri River where the town was to be located; Rudolph Hawpe, an early settler in Saline County, who owned a farm near Arrow Rock that became a popular camp meeting location; Reverend Peyton

Nowlin, a pioneer Baptist minister, had organized one of the first area churches, Zoar Baptist Church, in what is now the Hardeman neighborhood. Later, the church relocated to Jonesboro, where it still holds services; Benjamin Huston had a farm three miles west of Arrow Rock with his brother Joseph, who had served as one of the election judges for Arrow Rock Township as early as 1824. Joseph Huston was then the justice of the peace for the county and later became a county judge.

Records of town board meetings show that the village grew very slowly, but in spite of early difficulties, the cooperation of area residents and its favorable location helped the new village of Philadelphia survive. Captain William Becknell had moved to Saline County by 1827 and had served as justice of the peace. In 1828 and 1830 he was elected to the Missouri House of Representatives. Jerry Lecky and Frederick Hartgrove lived on the river in a log cabin called Ferry House and operated the ferry. In the spring of 1830, Andrew Brownlee, a carpenter, built a two-room house in the new town.

Some time between Christmas and New Year's Eve of 1829, Duke Paul of Wuerttemberg and his party, including Pomp Charbonneau, passed through the Boonslick region again, on Paul's second excursion to the far West. A descendant of the duke's, Prince Hans von Sachsen-Altenburg, has written an account of Pomp's seven years in Europe, traveling with Paul from court to court in Germany and visiting France and Spain. Now a young man of twenty-six, he was returning to the life he had known before he met Duke Paul. They were at the mouth of the Yellowstone River in May 1830, and in September they floated back downriver in a pirogue, bringing with them the duke's pet eagle.

A trapping, trading, and hunting expedition had left St. Louis on February 16, 1830. One participant, Warren Angus Ferris, wrote of passing through the Boonslick area:

> On 21st, we entered the eighteen-mile prairie, east of Franklin, beneath a bright sky and a balmy air. A few miles and the weather changed sadly, a terrible storm set in, which we were obliged to face and brave, for shelter was out of the question. . . . Two days after this we reached and passed through the village of Franklin, which a pitiless monster (The river) was in

the act of swallowing up. Near the village we met with innumerable flocks of paraquets—the first I had ever seen in the wild state—whose beautiful plumage of green and gold flashed above us like . . . gems.

Crossed the river at Arrow Rock ferry on the twenty-fifth.

Near the site of Fort Osage, William Clark had seen "Parrot queets" in June 1804, the earliest known sighting west of the Mississippi. J. K. Townsend wrote in his *Narrative of a Journey across the Rocky Mountains* that on April 7, 1833, he observed unusual birds at Boonville.

We saw here vast numbers of the beautiful Parrot of this country, the *Psittacus carolinensis*. They flew around us in flocks, keeping a constant and loud screaming, as though they would chide us for invading their territory, and the splendid green and red of their plumage glancing in the sunshine, as they whirled and circled within a few feet of us had a most magnificent appearance. They seemed entirely unsuspicious of danger, and after being fired at only huddled closer together as if to obtain protection from each other, and as their companions are falling around them, they curve down their necks and look at them fluttering upon the ground, as though perfectly at a loss to account for so unusual an occurrence. It is a most inglorious sort of shooting, downright, cold-blooded murder.

According to *Birds in Missouri,* published by the Missouri Department of Conservation, the bird, commonly known as the Carolina parakeet, which was once seen from the Atlantic Coast to the Rockies, was extinct in the U.S. by 1914.

In 1830 General Thomas A. Smith quit working at the land office in Franklin and moved to his property in Saline County. He called the seven thousand acres "Experiment, "because the land had never been farmed. According to Charles van Ravenswaay, Smith "succeeded in exploding the theory that prairie land was infertile." He became a successful farmer and stock raiser, but his decision to live in Saline County was probably largely responsible for the dealings his notorious brother John Smith T was to have in the county.

As a note in the *Missouri Historical Review* for April 1932 reported, Thomas Smith's older brother, John Smith T, "was credited with killing fifteen men, but 'he was as polished and courteous a gentle-man as ever lived in the state of Missouri' and 'as mild a mannered man as ever put a bullet into the human body.'" Dick Steward, author of *Frontier Swashbuckler: The Life and Legend of John Smith T,* says Thomas Smith's long-estranged brother became "intrigued by the flora and fauna of the Boonslick" and began to amass land in Saline County. The Thomas Smith family was not "all that enthralled" with Smith T's arrival in the county. His sister-in-law reportedly "once told family members that Jack 'should have been hung' for all the grief he inflicted."

Thomas Smith and John Smith T (who had added the "T" for Ten-nessee to distinguish himself from other men named John Smith) developed a plan to transport farm products from Experiment Farm to Smith T's Mine Shibboleth, near Potosi, in Washington County, and bring lead and other products back to the Boonslick. The plan was successful for a time, and Smith T also started a salt-producing operation south of present-day Marshall. Life near the river had its advantages for the "swashbuckler." His favorite method of trans-portation across the state was by pirogue. Steward wrote: "Even after steam boats began traffic on the river he preferred his own boat, manned by slaves and well fortified with provisions, arms and muni-tions. The *Kansas City Journal* noted that 'he traveled with all the splendor and ease of an Eastern Monarch.'" He also traveled by barge, occasionally stopping at riverside hotels or taverns, where most other travelers tried to stay out of his way, sometimes without success. In the 1830s a young James S. Rollins was in a Jefferson City hotel to give an address at a temperance rally when Smith T arrived on his barge. He insisted Rollins accept several drinks ("Drink or fight," he said, according to the story) before allowing him to depart and give his lecture on the evils of alcohol.

Historians question the truth of some of the stories that circulat-ed in nineteenth-century Missouri about Smith T's exploits, but one episode in his life is documented. He ran for governor in 1832 but lost to David Dunklin, a Potosi lawyer, by a large margin. Smith T received only about 314 votes in the state, not a single one of them in Saline County, where he owned extensive property.

Soon after John Sappington and his family's arrival in the area in

1817, his oldest daughter, Eliza, had married Alonzo Pearson, a merchant in Chariton. The couple had five children when Eliza found the legality of her marriage to be in question. According to Thomas Shackelford's "Early Recollections of Missouri," "a man by the name of Denison of Saline County was in the Pearson store in Chariton and heard him mention some incident that had taken place in Georgia." Denison accused him of being a man named Parsons who had a wife in Georgia. Pearson left the state, and Sappington sought an annulment for Eliza from the legislature, which refused at first until it could be assured of Eliza's wishes. Evidently she convinced the legislature, and in 1831 it awarded her a special divorce bill, the children, and all the family property. Shackelford said Pearson came back with a divorce decree in hand, and he and Eliza were remarried, but the feeling against him among family and friends was so strong that he left again for Texas, where he died shortly afterward. Sappington took responsibility for the care and education of the children. During this difficult time for the Sappingtons, eighteen-year-old Jane Sappington married Claiborne Fox Jackson, at that time a Franklin merchant. She died only five months later, while her father was still seeking a cure for the malarial fever from which she suffered.

According to Charles van Ravenswaay, when John Beauchamp Jones and his brother Joe came west to "Philadelphia" from Philadelphia, Pennsylvania, in 1830 to set up the first grocery store, the only residents of the village were a Canadian French trapper who had worked for General William Henry Ashley's company and his wife living in a mud shanty, and a "family from Virginia living in a log house with their slaves in a row of huts." Jones, an aspiring writer who used the pen name Luke Shortfield, recorded what he saw on the Missouri frontier. This was later included in a book of fiction, but his description rings true for the New Philadelphia of 1831.

> It was not long before I had explored every part of the town. The site was high and dry, but unfortunately broken up immensely by abrupt hills and deep hollows. With the exception of the road which led from the ferry to the prairie, and the small space of ground, some forty by twenty feet, on which the store was situ-

ated, and a few transverse deer paths, every foot of the town was covered with bushes, brambles and trees. And these in many parts were impenetrably united by complete webs of wild vines.

Jones described a frontier store in *The Western Merchant,* drawing the information, according to Lewis E. Atherton, from his own experience in Arrow Rock:

> Located in a clearing in the trees, where rattlesnakes and deer could be observed occasionally, the building appeared little different from the scattering of log-cabin homes. . . . In the salesroom . . . shelves ranged along all four sides. A counter of boards divided the salesroom. . . . A large shoebox or hat box served as a desk, and money was kept in a drawer under the counter . . . with a small hole cut through the top of the counter for convenience and safety when business was heavy.

The new merchants of the fledgling village welcomed travelers for the trade they brought.

Mormons, followers of Joseph Smith, began coming west in great numbers during the '30s, initially headed for Jackson County, Missouri, where a small group had settled in the winter of 1830–1831. During the next seven years, hundreds of Mormons poured through Arrow Rock, in spite of increasing violence against their settlements. Thomas Shackelford recalled that strangers were entertained gladly and without charge in Saline County, sometimes Mormons as well as others. "I well remember that Joseph Smith, the Mormon prophet, with Sydney Rigdon, came afoot to my mother's house, remained overnight, and gave my mother a Mormon bible, and I listened as the prophet told her of his interview with an angel who revealed to him the mysteries of the Book of Mormon."

When author Washington Irving returned to the United States in 1832 after seventeen years abroad, he traveled through the Boonslick country, accompanied by C. J. Latrobe, on a tour of the West. Irving later drew on their experiences for a book, and Latrobe kept a journal in which he recorded their crossing of the river: "The Missouri was . . . crossed at Arrow Rock Ferry, and our line of route then lay wholly to the south of the river. I recollect with delight our escape from a hot and crowded log-cabin, where we had been compelled to halt after dark, and pass a restless night, and the following morning's ride over the open prairies."

The following year an exploration up the river took place that some historians consider second in importance only to the Lewis and Clark expedition in the knowledge of the West that resulted. It was led by Maximilian, Prince of Weid-Neuweid, a German principality on the Weid River at its juncture with the Rhine near Coblenz. Maximilian had engaged Swiss artist Karl Bodmer to accompany him and had brought an assistant, David Dreidoppel, to gather scientific specimens. The youngest of eight children, with no family responsibilities, Maximilian had concentrated his studies on the natural sciences and had a reputation as a naturalist based on his report of a Brazilian expedition fifteen years earlier. He now wanted to study the Plains Indian tribes, for which he had prepared for years.

Like most foreign visitors, Maximilian had visited William Clark when he arrived in St. Louis, to inform him of his plans and get Clark's approval for the trip. Clark had given the prince his blessing and a map of the Lewis and Clark Voyage of Discovery, and the group set off on the American Fur Company's *Yellowstone,* on its third annual trip up the Missouri. As a scientist, Maximilian was primarily interested in getting to the Indian territory, but he did comment on a stop at the new town of Philadelphia:

> April 14, 1833: We lay for the night at Arrow Rock, a chain in which flint is found, of which the Indians formerly made the heads of their arrows. In a ravine, before Arrow Rock Hill, there is a new village, which is called New Philadelphia though the inhabitants do not approve of this name. On the following morning proceeding on our voyage, we passed little Arrow Rock, and found a very fertile and rather populous country.

Maximilian's account of the year he spent among the Plains Indians, *Travels in the Interior of America,* is a major contribution to the history of the West, and his field notes, translated from the German years later, are of even greater importance. Bodmer's engravings are considered "masterpieces of ethnographic" reporting, and together

AGED 59.
1834.

☺ John Sappington's experiments with quinine saved many lives, but the medical community did not accept his discoveries. George Caleb Bingham painted his portrait in 1834. (Missouri Department of Natural Resources, courtesy State Historical Soceity of Missouri, Columbia)

text and engravings constitute, many historians believe, "an unmatched record of early trans-Mississippi exploration."

Upriver a young company clerk, Alexander Culbertson, gave a description of Maximilian. He was "very well preserved and able to endure considerable fatigue. He was a man of medium height, sans teeth, passionately fond of his pipe . . . speaking very broken English. His favorite dress was a white slouch hat, a black velvet coat, rather rusty from long service, and probably the greasiest pair of trousers that ever encased princely legs." At Fort Clark, Maximilian encountered Toussaint Charbonneau, who served as his guide and entertained him with stories of his adventures. When Maximilian returned to New Philadelphia thirteen months later, residents had decided to rename their village Arrow Rock.

The first great demand for Sappington's medical expertise had come in the summer of 1833, when the first case of cholera occurred in the area. Sappington and his new partner, George Penn, who had joined his practice in 1832, advised and treated patients hour after hour and day after day. Compounding the dangers of cholera was a possible misunderstanding of its cause. Some thought the disease was being carried by riverboats since incidents of the cholera epidemics seemed to follow navigable streams. The cause was actually food or water contaminated with the bacteria *Vibrio cholerae.* Preventive measures included improving sanitation, particularly preventing sewage from contaminating drinking water. Symptoms of cholera were profuse, watery diarrhea, and often vomiting, beginning one to five days after infection. The consequences were rapid dehydration and often death.

Doctors gave patients laudanum and essence of peppermint to stop the diarrhea. In addition, they encouraged patients to "eat and drink as usual and try to keep up with their regular activities, but in moderation, and to remain cheerful." According to Sappington only three lives were lost out of eighty confirmed cases in the area during 1833 and 1835. He noted in *The Theory and Treatment of Fevers:* "The same year that cholera raged here it also raged at St. Louis and in other parts of the State with its usual fatality—under the common treatment of bleeding, puking, and purging . . . at least three-fourths, if not more of the cases proved fatal." Sappington continued to experiment with the proper dose of quinine to treat fevers, treating himself and willing patients until he developed a satisfactory dosage.

Despite all the challenges, social events and progress continued. In September 1833 the Sappington home was again the scene of a wedding when Louisa, eighteen-year-old daughter of John Sappington, married Claiborne Fox Jackson, the widower of her sister, Jane. In 1834, Judge Joseph Huston built a two-and-half-story brick building in Arrow Rock on four lots he had purchased for eighty-nine dollars the preceding year. It soon housed travelers. William Price came to

Ⓠ John Locke Hardeman was one of the most successful planters of his time, and like many of his neighbors, he had his portrait painted by George Caleb Bingham. (State Historical Society of Missouri, Columbia)

Arrow Rock from Maryland to practice medicine in the mid-1830s. He married Mary Ellen Sappington, another of John's daughters, and in 1838 became a partner in the business, which Sappington began that year—selling quinine pills under the label of "Dr. John Sappington's Anti-Fever Pills." Quinine use for malaria was not readily accepted, but one historian suggests "the new name may have helped sales and, consequently, cures." Between fifteen and thirty salesmen on horseback, many of them Sappington family members or slaves, peddled Sappington's Anti-Fever Pills across the South and West. Sappington or his sons rode to Philadelphia to get the hundreds of pounds of quinine needed.

The Sappingtons' business was not the only one to prosper. John Locke Hardeman continued to experiment with farming methods. He invented a horse-drawn machine to cut hemp and worked on one that harvested grain. Cyrus McCormick, who ultimately claimed the credit for the revolutionary invention, spent a week on the Hardeman farm before he patented his reaping machine in 1834.

Interest in the Santa Fe Trail had continued. In 1831 Alphonso Wetmore, a lawyer and compiler of the first *Gazetteer of Missouri,* responded to questions from Senator Benton about the increase in trade: "In 1821, the caravan consisted of 21 men and their merchandise was valuated at $3,000. The caravan of last spring numbered 260 men, with 135 wagons and merchandise in the amount of $270,000." The following spring, Mary Dodson Donoho, then living in Columbia, became the first Anglo-American woman to travel the Santa Fe Trail, joining her husband, William Donoho, and about 180 other Missouri adventurers. The Donohos had their nine-month-old daughter with them.

Because of Indian attacks on an earlier caravan, Congress had established a regiment of U.S. Mounted Rangers to escort the train of more than a hundred wagons and carriages, which carried more than $100,000 worth of goods. The expedition slogged through almost continuous rain, and one historian observes that Mary Donoho would have been grateful for the good drinking water it provided. Except for the rain, the trip to Santa Fe was uneventful, and the caravan arrived there in August 1832. When it returned to Missouri, the Donohos remained in Santa Fe, where they opened a hotel, LaFonda, on the plaza. Another daughter, Harriet Donoho, was the first Anglo child born in Santa Fe, and a son, James, followed. The Donohos remained in Santa Fe for five years, but when a rebellion against the governor began, they joined a caravan to return to Missouri in 1837, bringing three white women who had been captured in Texas by Comanches. William Donoho had ransomed the women, and the Donohos returned them to their families. They settled in Clarksville, Texas, where Mary died in 1880.

In the spring of 1835 Swiss adventurer Johann August Sutter joined a caravan organized in St. Louis for a trip to Santa Fe. Supported and outfitted by friends, he invested in old pistols, "cheap trinkets, and jackets of former German students in St. Louis pawnshops," which he sold in Taos and Santa Fe, bringing back mules and wine. For his second trip in 1836, he persuaded more than a dozen German immigrants to join him, but that undertaking was a failure, and most investors lost their funds. Sutter went to California, where a decade later, the discovery of gold on his property led to the gold rush.

Saline County resident George Caleb Bingham had developed a local reputation as a portraitist by the early 1830s and had painted some of the elite of Arrow Rock, including Dr. and Mrs. John Sappington. In 1834 he moved to Columbia, where he met attorney James S. Rollins, who was to become his lifelong friend and supporter. With Rollins's encouragement Bingham went to St. Louis to set up a studio, but soon became discouraged and in May 1835, he headed back west on a steamboat. According to historian Kenneth Winn, he became ill on the trip "with what has variously been called smallpox, or the measles. Although Bingham recovered, his hair did not, and proud and vain man that he was he wore a wig for the rest of his life." Bingham was back in St. Louis in the winter of 1835–1836, but after he married Sarah Elizabeth Hutchison, he settled for a while in Arrow Rock.

Residents and newcomers to Arrow Rock continued to establish shops and businesses despite the hard times. H. S. Wilhelm came to Arrow Rock in 1836 and opened a tailor shop. He served on the town board for nineteen years, twelve as the chairman. Many of the town elections were held in his shop. Isaac Neff (the name had been Nave until some members of the family changed the spelling) built a tavern on the Santa Fe Trail about six miles west of Arrow Rock, a log building with a shake roof. Travelers slept in one large loft. The Santa Fe Trail went between the tavern and Neff's barn, and the tavern soon became a station and post office.

Throughout the 1830s, religious groups were active in the Arrow Rock area. Several country churches such as Zoar Baptist Church near the Hardeman farm and Concord Baptist Church in Cox's Bottom were thriving, led by ministers such as Reverend Thomas

Kinney, who was preaching to settlers in the future Saline County as early as 1816, and Reverend Peyton Nowlin, who came soon after. The Methodist Episcopals organized in Arrow Rock as early as 1831, only two years after the village got its start, and in 1835 the village was the location of a notable conference held by the Methodist Episcopal Church. According to William B. Napton's 1910 *Past and Present of Saline County Missouri:*

> Over a hundred preachers were present in Arrow Rock for a conference of the Methodist Episcopal church for the district. The boundaries of the conference extended south to the Arkansas line, and there were ministers present from all parts of the district. During the session there was an average daily attendance of a thousand people, a large concourse for that period. The conference lasted ten days, and the interest manifested was taken advantage of by the zealous ministers present, and many additions to the church were made. The venerable Bishop Roberts presided, and the services were for the most part very impressive. Many in attendance had never before seen a real live bishop, and the occasion was long remembered. Among those in attendance were many Christianized Indians from the territory afterwards called Kansas, the Delaware, Wyandot, Shawnee and Kickapoos. Clad in their Indian costume and paying close attention to the services, they were objects of much attention. This conference was remembered by the people for many years afterwards.

Many residents of the Boonslick became alarmed about Mormon settlements in Missouri. Lilburn Boggs, a former resident of Franklin, assistant factor of Fort Osage, and Independence businessman, had been elected governor of Missouri in 1836. He was well known in western Missouri, and when he gave the infamous order on October 24, 1838, that the Mormons must be treated as enemies, "exterminated or driven from the state," militia members from Saline County were among those who participated in the "Mormon War." Hostilities were intensified by rumors that the Mormons were abolitionists, and many fled farther west. It took more than a hundred years for Missouri to rescind Governor Boggs's order: On June 25, 1976, Governor Christopher S. Bond issued an executive order, "Expressing on behalf of all Missourians our deep regret for the injustice and suffering which was caused by this Order No. 44, dated October 27, 1838, issued by Governor Lilburn W. Boggs."

The population of Saline County grew rapidly from 1830 to 1840 when the census reported 3,635 residents, including 1,615 slaves, in the county. In *Agriculture and Slavery in Missouri's Little Dixie,* Douglas Hurt points out that while the white population increased by 69 percent in the decade, the number of slaves increased by 129 percent. In 1830 most slaveholders owned one to ten slaves, with only four persons owning twenty or more. By 1840 five Saline County slaveholders owned more than twenty slaves, and two had more than sixty. Reports of crimes both by and against slaves increased as the population increased. In April 1841 a slave named Rachael belonging to Thomas B. Finley died as a result of repeated beatings. Finley's family, who lived in Blackwater, buried Rachael on his property on April 13, the day after she died, but they made no attempt to hide her death and sent for neighbors, who apparently notified the authorities. Rachael's body was disinterred and autopsied on April 18. The coroner testified that Rachael had died of a ruptured blood vessel brought on by a severe beating, and Finley was summoned to appear before the circuit court in Saline County to answer charges of second-degree murder or manslaughter. Harriet Frazier, who researched the case for her book, *Slavery and Crime in Missouri, 1773–1865,* could find no record of the settlement of the case, but she notes that this case and others showed "community disapproval of [such an] act."

Arrow Rock served as the Saline County seat during 1839–1840, but Marshall, located centrally in the county, became the permanent county seat in 1840. Napton mentions one effect this had on Arrow Rock: "The Santa Fe Trail, crossing the river at Arrow Rock, [had] followed the old Osage Trace in a direct route across the county to Grand Pass until after the location of the county seat at Marshall. . . . It then changed to pass through Marshall, and traffic at the Arrow Rock crossing slowed." Arrow Rock nevertheless continued to grow, and newcomers such as Charles M. Bradford and William Price built or rebuilt homes that became showplaces. Bradford had come from New York City to the Arrow Rock area in 1840. In 1841 he bought a

ⓢ The Saline County Courthouse was built in 1839, when Arrow Rock was the county seat. One room served as the courtroom; the other was a bedroom, where the judge could stay while in town. Early judges served several counties and traveled from place to place—along a circuit—to hold court. This 1931 photo shows the building before it was restored by the Friends of Arrow Rock. (State Historical Society of Missouri, Columbia)

frame house at the corner of Main and Sixth Streets, which he enlarged. He married Lavinia Pearson, a granddaughter of John Sappington. Price and his wife, Mary Ellen Sappington, built a two-story brick home at Seventh and Main Streets.

Joseph Huston built a warehouse on the riverbank for the increasing trade. He also officially opened a tavern "to accommodate the travelers headed west—a place for weary travelers to eat and sleep—and possibly to drink." In a letter published many years later in the *Saline County Index,* Glen O. Hardeman wrote:

> On my first visit to Saline in 1840 I landed at Arrow Rock from
> a steam boat, in the night, and as I intended going to the coun-

try early in the morning, I took lodgings only, at the hotel kept by that well-known and popular citizen, Joseph Huston, Sr., for which I was charged the sum of 12 1/2 cents, or, I should say, a "bit." On my return in a few days I dined at the same hotel and was charged another "bit" for an excellent dinner.

In the early 1840s Huston constructed a two-story brick addition to the original two-and-a-half-story Federal-style brickhouse; he used the first floor as a general store. Although gold and silver were accepted as payment, generally people traded furs, lard, eggs, and even livestock for items they wished to purchase. The store also served as the post office. The second floor, which could be reached from the street by an outside staircase, was a large room where meetings and dances could be held. A stonemason, Burton Godsey, was hired by the town board to try to connect the Main Street with the area at the base of the bluff where a wharf and Huston's warehouses were located.

Meanwhile, anyone in the state who wanted to participate in the activities of the Missouri Democratic party was encouraged to visit John Sappington. Sappington, along with his family, friends, and neighbors, who also owned many thousands of acres in the area— Thomas A. Smith, John Locke Hardeman, county judge Thomas Shackelford, and Sappington sons-in-law Marmaduke and Claiborne Fox Jackson—became known across the state as the "Central Clique," with influence across Missouri and the nation. Missouri's first senator, Thomas Hart Benton, Sappington's longtime friend, often visited. Benton supported causes that benefited the common man, such as giving unpurchased western land to poor farmers. A strong state rights advocate, he wished to unify the South and West by promoting agriculture. The clique agreed and conferred about these and other issues of the day, becoming increasingly influential in the politics of the new state. In 1840 Marmaduke was elected lieutenant governor to serve with Governor Thomas Reynolds of Fayette. Sappington had become a wealthy landowner, with enormous political power, but although his sons, Darwin and William Breathitt, built elaborate homes, he continued to live modestly in Pilot Hickory.

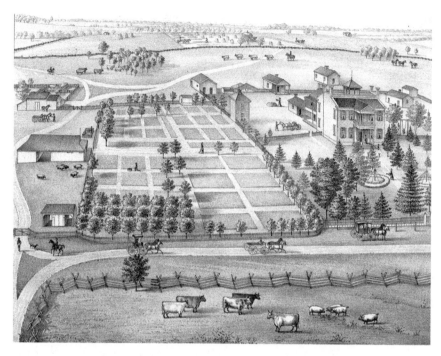

Prairie Park. William Breathitt Sappington, John Sappington's son, built this estate near Arrow Rock in 1844. There is evidence his father thought it unduly extravagant. Tours of Prairie Park can be arranged through Friends of Arrow Rock. (State Historical Society of Missouri, Columbia)

On an 1842 visit to Missouri, Kit Carson had traveled to St. Louis before deciding to go back west. On the deck of a steamer going upriver, he met Lieutenant John Charles Frémont, who had secretly married Jesse Benton the previous year. Although disapproving of the marriage originally, Senator Benton had reconciled himself to his new son-in-law and decided to send him on an expedition west. Learning of the planned expedition, Kit reported in his memoirs that he "informed him I could guide him to any point he would wish to go. He replied he would make inquiries [regarding me]. He done so." Frémont was impressed with the young guide. He wrote, "On the boat I met Kit Carson . . . I was pleased with him and his manner of address at this first meeting. He was a man of . . . frank speech and address; quiet and unassuming. . . . I had expected to engage as guide an old mountaineer, Captain Drips, but I was so pleased with Carson that . . . I was glad to take him."

Frémont's report that the South Pass in the Wind River Mountains could be easily traveled by wagons helped to encourage further American immigration to the Oregon Country. A second expedition in 1843–1844 completed the exploration of the Oregon Trail. The Frémonts' report of the first two expeditions, enlivened by Jesse's colorful style, brought national attention to Kit Carson and led to a long and lasting friendship between him and the Frémonts.

The Masonic Lodge in Arrow Rock, founded in 1842, served both travelers and townspeople. Records indicate that many who moved west were Masons, and Arrow Rock resident H. S. Mills was presented with a certificate of membership before he traveled to Santa Fe. Another attraction in the community was a "Female Academy," founded by Reverend G. Hickman in 1843. Housed in a brick building that had originally been the Arrow Rock Academy and advertised by Hickman with flyers and newspaper notices, the school flourished.

Notable people continued to visit or pass by the small village on the Missouri River halfway across the state. In 1843 John James Audubon, a naturalist famous for his study of birds and animals and for the book *Birds of America,* visited the area after hearing reports of Washington Irving's travels. Audubon traveled on the steamer *Omega,* which was carrying supplies for trading posts belonging to Pierre Chouteau Jr. According to Captain Joseph La Barge Jr., who was on the boat, he had a party of five assistants and hunters that had been provided by Chouteau. La Barge reported that Audubon "made a very fine collection of animals during the voyage, as we had taken on special hunters to assist him. Mr. Audubon himself was a dead shot and remarkable for his powers of endurance for his age." Although Audubon "would occasionally ask questions about the country, climate, and animals and birds that were likely to be seen on such a voyage," La Barge considered him "very reserved, I might almost say overbearing." The *Omega* returned to St. Louis in June, but the Audubon party remained at the Yellowstone until autumn and then returned downriver "in a Makinaw boat, accompanied by Kenon Provost, the first white man that crossed the Rockies through South Pass."

In 1843 George Caleb Bingham's young wife, Elizabeth, then living with her parents in Boonville, wrote her husband about the possibility of moving back to Arrow Rock. After the birth of their son Isaac Newton in 1837, they had built a Federal-style brick home on a lot in Arrow Rock that Bingham had bought from Claiborne Fox Jackson. Since Bingham had cabinetmaking and carpentry skills, historians believe he may have built or completed finishing work on the house himself. Elizabeth was staying with her parents in Boonville while Bingham traveled to find work, but they still owned the house.

While traveling in the East, Bingham had become interested in "genre" paintings, which showed realistic scenes of everyday life. He continued painting portraits of friends and well-known public figures, but he did not forget the new style that had caught his eye. He had moved his family to Washington, D.C., in 1840, planning to study the work of eastern artists and paint portraits of political leaders. When Newton died the following year, Bingham's wife and second son, Horace, returned to Missouri for the winter. Bingham wrote sadly that he believed Newton would rather have "fallen asleep in a corner of his little garden in Arrow Rock." But as a portrait painter he had to find subjects and could not settle back in Arrow Rock, however much he might have wished to do so. Yet while he continued painting to support his family, he returned to Missouri when he could, drawn partly by his growing interest in politics. Bingham sometimes struggled to ignore that interest, but by 1840, he had become involved. That year he was commissioned to paint a banner and invited to make a speech supporting the Whigs. He wrote his longtime friend James Rollins in Columbia, that he must leave his painter's life and take a stand against "corruption, tyranny, and threats to liberty," which he considered were being made by Thomas Hart Benton, Missouri's longtime senator, and Benton's Democratic party. Instead of giving up painting, Bingham began using art in the political arena. In response to Elizabeth's wish to move back to Arrow Rock, however, Bingham wrote to her, "It would be hard for me to tell now when we shall want our house to dwell in ourselves. I fear it will be many years, unless a great change should take place in my pursuits and feelings."

Meanwhile, after his travels in Europe, Pomp Charbonneau soon adapted well to his old life in the West, where he was known as John B. Charbonneau. In *Interpreters with Lewis and Clark,* historian W. Dale Nelson reports that in 1833 Pomp was at a trade rendezvous on the Green River in present-day Wyoming, interpreting for the Shoshone and Jim Bridger, who had first gone west as one of "Ashley's Hundred." In the late 1830s he was hunting buffalo with Kit Carson near Bent's Fort in present-day Colorado. In 1842, on his first expedition west, John Charles Frémont met Jim Beckwourth, who took him to Charbonneau's camp on an island in the Platt. Water was low in the Platt, and he was waiting for spring rains to make it possible to take a load of furs to St. Louis. He made a mint julep for Frémont and treated his visitors to "boiled beef tongue and coffee with sugar." The next year he was on the Oregon Trail with the hunting party of Scottish nobleman Sir William Drummond Stewart. The explorer William Sublette was the guide and Charbonneau the driver for the party.

A decade after his return from Europe, Charbonneau was considered "the best man on foot on the plains or in the Rocky Mountains." A few years later he was described as one of the "most knowledgeable [guides] in all of New Mexico." When Stephen Kearny was trying to find a wagon route to the Pacific in 1845, he signed on as a guide on an expedition to occupy New Mexico and California. Kearny assigned him to a Mormon Battalion led by Captain Ste. George Cooke, where he proved of great value in "selecting routes, trapping beaver, finding water, establishing camps, discovering passes, scouting, and . . . hunting."

In 1844 John and Nannie Sites moved to Arrow Rock. Historian Robert L. Dyer wrote that John's father, John P. Sites Sr., had established a gunshop in Boonville in 1835. The young couple had been married only three years, and John had first set up and operated a gunsmith shop in Clifton, in Cooper County. Since many settlers continued to pass through Arrow Rock on the trails west, the new location provided more opportunity, and Sites had a profitable business. A working gun was essential for settlers on the frontier. A gun might cost as much as $50, at a time when a wagon cost $60, and land could be purchased for $1.25 an acre. Gunowners also had to

Meredith Miles Marmaduke became Missouri's eighth governor. (State Historical Society of Missouri, Columbia)

purchase shot, percussion caps, lead, and powder. A gunsmith was an important tradesman in a town, and John and Nannie were a valuable addition to the life of Arrow Rock.

Sappington published *The Theory and Treatment of Fevers* in 1844, the first medical book published west of the Mississippi River. It made his formula for quinine treatment available to the world, which meant competition for the business he had developed. According to a biography of Sappington published by the Friends of Arrow Rock, he was, perhaps, protesting the extravagance of his sons, who had built large homes as the family prospered. In spite of his success, the medical establishment continued to disagree with Sappington's practices, and he was denied membership in the St.

Louis Medical Society, later incorporated as the Medical Society of Missouri. Perhaps the fact that his daughter became first lady of the State of Missouri the same year helped him overlook this slight.

Early in 1844, Missouri newspapers ran a headline announcing that Lieutenant Governor Meredith Miles Marmaduke of Arrow Rock had become governor of the state. After serving three years as governor, Thomas Reynolds committed suicide in the governor's home in Jefferson City on February 9, 1844. Marmaduke's wife Lavinia, daughter of John Sappington, became the first lady of the state. Since only nine months remained in the term, and their eighth child was less than two years old, the family may not have made the move to the governor's mansion, which was then a two-story residence on the same block as the capitol.

Prior to his Missouri-based trading experience, treks to Santa Fe, inclusion in the political clique at the Sappingtons', and service to Saline County as judge and surveyor, Marmaduke had become uniquely qualified for high political office. His parents, both born in England, had received a grant of the entire county of Westmoreland, Virginia, where they became the owners of many slaves and developed a large estate. Marmaduke, born in Virginia in 1791, received a good education, and served as deputy U.S. marshal and recorder of the county. At the age of twenty, he raised a regiment of soldiers for the War of 1812 with England, was chosen colonel, and "rendered valiant and courageous service." Even though Governor Marmaduke was recognized as "an able and efficient servant of the people," he lost his party's nomination for governor in 1844 to John C. Edwards of Cole County and returned to his family home near Arrow Rock.

Chapter 5

Developing Center
1844–1859

In the 1840s, severe flooding and new business opportunities brought more settlers to the Arrow Rock community, and landowners acquired increasing numbers of slaves. John Sappington's medical successes and the political involvement of his sons and neighbors continued to bring prominence to the area, as did the successes of local artist George Caleb Bingham. The discovery of gold in California drew thousands of people to the West. Like other explorers and immigrants before them, they passed through the village. Arrow Rock prospered, but many Saline County residents had to seek higher lands in the summer of 1844. According to the 1881 *History of Saline County, Missouri:*

> The weather was very peculiar. It rained a veritable "forty days and forty nights." Every evening out of a clear sky just as the sun went down there arose a dark, ominous looking cloud in the northwest. Flashes of lightning and the heaviest thunder followed, and about ten o'clock the rain would begin to fall in torrents. The bridges were nearly all washed away. . . . The bottoms were all overflown, and the citizens were forced to leave them and retreat to the higher lands. This rise far exceeded that of 1826—some settlers say by ten feet. Crowds of people gathered on the shores [of the Missouri] to view the sights presented upon . . . the mighty river. Houses and wrecks of various other kinds of building floated along; dead animals were common; there were haystacks, or remnants of them, as well as corn-

shocks; white rails, boards, timbers, and even household furniture. . . . One instance is related, where there was borne upon the current . . . a stable, upon which were a number of chickens, alive and doing as well as could be expected. One old cock stood bravely up and crew lustily, and even defiantly, as if he were master of the situation after all.

The Sappington family and Claiborne Fox Jackson had suffered more tragedy in the 1830s. Louisa, the second of Sappington's daughters to marry Jackson, had been killed in a runaway horse accident in May 1838, and her baby boy died only a month later. Two children, both under four years of age, were left motherless. A few months later, Jackson married Eliza Sappington Pearson, a third Sappington daughter. In addition to her own five children, Eliza became mother to her sister's children while Jackson was serving his first term in the Missouri general assembly.

From earliest settlement, the economy of the Arrow Rock area had depended on slave labor, and Saline County's deepest concern seemed to be keeping the area's slaves in line. As midcentury approached, nearly half the population was black. Slave auctions took place on the Arrow Rock Tavern steps, and local laws similar to those established by the state regulated activities of slaves:

* Slaves out after 10:00 p.m. without a pass were to be punished by ten lashes.
* It was against the law for slaves to learn to read or write.
* A white man had to be present at all meetings of slaves, including church.
* Slaves could not testify against a white man in court.
* Slaves could not legally marry.

Because slaves could not legally marry, and children born to an enslaved woman belonged to her owner, slave families could be separated whenever it suited the owner's purpose. Dick Green, according to his great-grandson Fielding Draffen, was a young boy when he came to Missouri via several rivers, "and . . . got off the boat in Arrow Rock in Saline County, Mo, as a slave." Draffen, writing a letter published in the fall 1995 *Mid-Missouri Black Watch*, told Dick Green's story: "One day, somewhere in Virginia, a white man told him to get on a wagon and go with it to help unload it. That was the last time he saw his mother, sisters, and brothers. He had been sold."

Draffen, who founded the Missouri Negro High School Reunion Association, remembered that "Grandpa Dick had blue eyes and 'straight' hair. He . . . was pretty sure his father was also his previous slave master, hence the reason he was cruelly separated from his family. . . . So Grandpa Dick did not like to be reminded of his light skin, blue eyes and 'straight' hair because it reminded him of the people who cruelly separated him from his loved ones."

Thomas Shackelford wrote that his mother "called my attention to the fact that sons in good families, as well as husbands, were having children by the slave women, that this social evil was bad enough among free people, but among bond women was terrible." Many citizens regarded slavery as a "necessary evil" for the economy, and most of the voters in Saline County supported the South, its causes, and its candidates, including the Central Clique of the Boonslick region.

John Sappington's financial success, phenomenal for the time and place, depended on slave labor. On his seven thousand acres, his twenty-plus slaves and tenants raised wheat, corn, and tobacco. He traded in mules, cattle, sheep, and hogs, and bought the first McCormick reaper in the county. Having experienced success with the marketing of the Anti-Fever Pills, agricultural ventures, and extensive money lending, he dissolved John Sappington and Sons in 1845 and reorganized into five companies operated by his sons, sons-in-law, and associates. "Dr. Bradford and Pearson Children" was established for the support of his daughter Eliza's children.

Sappington supported and educated Eliza's children even after her marriage to Jackson. Jackson's biographer, Christopher Phillips, notes that he never adopted the children and submitted bills for their support to Sappington. William Price, another Sappington son-in-law, became the manager of the production and packaging of the pills. Richard Marshall, a hunting companion of Jackson's who farmed and raised cattle, became Sappington's slave overseer. Historians credit Marshall and Sappington as the first men to sow bluegrass in the area. They seeded not only their pastures, but also roadsides.

Ⓢ Many farmers employed overseers to see that slaves worked steadily
and had no opportunity to escape. (State Historical Society of Missouri,
Columbia)

The Sappingtons organized a sixth company—John Sappington
and Company, Blacksmithing—the following year. The entire region
was growing; businesses, professional offices, and schools sprang up
to meet the needs of the people. Benjamin Townsend, son of early
settler Saunders Townsend, opened a dry goods store. Matthew Walton
Hall came to Arrow Rock in 1845. Around 1846 he built a home north
of the Arrow Rock businesses and soon became prominent in local
affairs, serving as one of the original trustees of the court-appointed
town board.

Still active in local Missouri affairs, Senator Thomas Hart Benton
continued his support of westward expansion and policies aimed at
helping the common man. He favored gold and silver currency over

paper and distrusted banks and corporations. The increasingly wealthy members of the Central Clique agreed with these policies, and Benton and other important Democrats attended many Sappington events, social as well as political. The Sappington family's political influence reached to the nation's capital.

However, as the 1844 election approached, the immediate annexation of Texas was proposed. Fearing an unnecessary war with Mexico, Benton opposed the move, which cost him support among the transplanted southerners in mid-Missouri. As tension between northern and southern states intensified, Benton's primary concern became keeping the union together, as Perry McCandless explains in the *Dictionary of Missouri Biography*:

> Benton foresaw the danger of the Union being dissolved over the slavery controversy, and, as the decade proceeded, he concluded that southern extremists posed the greatest danger to the nation. Turning his primary attention to the preservation of the Union, Benton became less a Missouri senator and more a national statesman, less a western man and more a nationalist.

When the Binghams returned to Missouri in 1844 they stayed with family or rented places to live. Whatever the reason for their return, Bingham was soon painting banners for the delegates from Boone, Howard, and Cooper counties to the Whig convention in Boonville. While still accepting commissions for political banners and portraits, George Caleb Bingham ran for the Missouri Legislature from Saline County on the Whig party ticket in 1846. He was perhaps looking for reasons to stay in the area as well as to have an opportunity to influence the state's political future. Although Bingham won the election by three votes, his opponent, Darwin Sappington, challenged the outcome, leaving the legislature to make the selection. The heavily Democratic legislature awarded the seat to Sappington.

Although he wanted to stay in the Boonslick area, Bingham had to return to the East to make a living with his paintings. There, studying drawings he had made in Missouri, he began to work on scenes depicting Missouri landscapes and the daily lives of Americans and Indians. Perhaps inspiration for the latter came from his childhood, when Indians still hunted in the Boonslick area. As late as 1838 an encampment of four or five hundred Osage Indians had located a few miles northwest of Arrow Rock for a time. Also numerous bands of Iowa, Sauk, and Fox, with occasional Kickapoo and Kaw, hunted in the area.

The spring of 1846, according to Francis Parkman Jr., was a busy one for the city of St. Louis, causing increased activity in the villages and towns like Arrow Rock along the Missouri River. As Parkman wrote in his classic history of the Oregon Trail, "Emigrants from every part of the country" were in St. Louis preparing for the "journey to Oregon and California," and "an unusual number of traders were making ready wagons and outfits for Santa Fe." Parkman and Quincy A. Shaw, a friend and relative, left St. Louis on the *Radner* on April 28 on "a tour of curiosity and amusement to the Rocky Mountains."

The *Radner* was loaded until the "water broke alternately over her guards." Her upper deck held "large weapons of a peculiar form" for the Santa Fe trade; equipment and provisions of a party of Oregon emigrants, a band of mules and horses, "a small French cart, of the sort . . . called a 'mule killer' beyond the frontier," and an assortment of boxes and barrels, saddles and harnesses, and other articles. "The passengers on board . . . corresponded with the freight. . . . Santa Fe traders, gamblers, speculators, and adventurers of various descriptions were in the cabin, and her steerage was crowded with Oregon emigrants, 'mountain men,' Negroes, and a party of Kansas Indians, who had been on a visit to St. Louis."

The Missouri was high that spring, and the *Radner* struggled against the strong current, "grating upon snags and hanging up for two or three hours at a time on sand-bars." It was not until the autumn, when they descended the river, that Parkman saw how dangerous the trip upriver had been. The water was low and "all the secrets of its treacherous shallows were exposed to view . . . broken trees . . . firmly embedded in the sand, and all pointing downstream, ready to impale any unhappy steamboat that at high water should pass over that dangerous ground."

The Missouri River was still the fastest, least-expensive route to travel, and in October 1848, John Charles Frémont, now a civilian, and his party left St. Louis by steamboat for Kansas City and then traveled to Westport to organize his fourth expedition. Kit Carson had scouted for the first expedition in 1842, the second in 1843–1844, and the third in 1845-1846, all sponsored by the U.S. government, and Carson had joined the revolt of American settlers against Mexican authorities at the outbreak of the Mexican War. Frémont's appointment as temporary military governor of California in 1847 had led to conflict with Stephen Kearny and a widely publicized court-martial in Washington for disobeying Kearny's orders. Frémont resigned from the army and undertook two privately supported expeditions seeking an all-weather central route for a railroad to the Pacific. For the 1848 expedition, he left without a scout. Some historians believe he hoped to engage Carson when he reached Taos, but he pressed on without a guide and at Pueblo found William Sherley Williams, now called "Old Bill" Williams, who was there recovering from a wound.

Old Bill had been with Frémont's third expedition for a while but had turned back when the explorer decided to cross the Great Salt Lake desert. Frémont's fourth expedition would be Williams's last. Heavy snows and severe cold made the passage Frémont selected through the La Garita Mountains impassable. Unable to go on, the thirty-two men in the expedition divided into three parties and tried to make their way back to Taos. Twenty-one survived. Frémont blamed Williams for the disaster, writing Jessie that "the error of our journey was committed in engaging this man." Some of his contemporaries and later historians suggest that Frémont himself was at fault for attempting the trip in the dead of winter and then ignoring the advice of his scout. About two months after the survivors reached Taos, Old Bill agreed to go back along the trail to try to recover baggage and instruments left behind by the struggling party. According to Alpheus Favour, he was killed by the Utes on March 19, 1849. Favour believes the Utes did not recognize him and reports that they gave him a chief's burial, but later findings cast doubt on this account of his death. William Brandon wrote, "As befits a folk hero, he simply vanished in the mountain mists." In any case, "During his own time, nearly anyone in the mountains who could write made some mention of him." The old scout was remembered in Arrow Rock and won praise from many, including Robert Wilson of Saline County,

George Caleb Bingham completed *The Stump Orator* in 1848. Many of the subjects were well known in the Boonslick and throughout the state. The painting was lost but a tintype survives. (State Historical Society of Missouri, Columbia)

who had known him and declared that "the river and mountain [in Arizona] . . . named in memory of his greatness . . . was a fitting tribute for a great scout."

While Frémont was on his unsuccessful expeditions, George Caleb Bingham was enjoying increasing success. He continued to travel and paint, and as Arrow Rock commissioner from 1846–1848, he enlisted area residents to pose for him. Oscar Potter, then in his teens, was among those whose likeness Bingham included in *The Stump Orator,* Bingham's first painting relating to politics as it was practiced in small towns throughout the state. In 1848, the year he completed *The Stump Orator,* Bingham won a seat as state representative. Politically he was moving closer to the pro-union views of Thomas Hart Benton as he continued to work on the election series of paintings. *Canvassing for a Vote* depicts men discussing politics in front of a brick building that critics believe was the Arrow Rock Tavern. His successes that year were marred once again by tragedy. His wife and baby son, Joseph, died in late 1848 and were buried in the Arrow Rock Cemetery.

Suffering a loss of another kind, John Locke Hardeman was forced to settle elsewhere when Fruitage Farm flooded. He chose a location in Saline County just west of Arrow Rock, where he again developed a botanical show garden. Hardeman bought three thousand acres in Saline, Howard, and Pettis counties. Lacking the wanderlust of the other Hardemans, he had remained single and dedicated to experimental farming and to rearing his younger brother Glen. He encouraging Glen to study medicine and set up practice in Arrow Rock.

In his message to Congress in December 1848, President James K. Polk confirmed the rumors that had reached Missouri about the discovery of gold at Sutter's Fort in California the previous January. The gold rush that resulted was to affect Arrow Rock as well as the rest of the nation. In 1849 Oscar Potter wrote to his uncle in Iowa:

> We have a mania raging here that has overspread our whole country. That is the California Gold fever. We hear nothing else talked about . . . no one wants to go anywhere but there. The organ of Aquisitiveness appears to have got the complete sway . . . the idea of picking up gold by the ounce takes almost everyone's fancy.

Oscar did not make the trip, but Glen Hardeman, along with 150 others from the county, caught "gold fever" and set off for California. The excitement grew as thousands of forty-niners took to the Santa Fe Trail.

The year brought trouble as well as visions of wealth. In the same 1849 letter, Oscar Potter wrote to his uncle:

> I suppose that you have all heard of the near approach of the cholera and of course [we] prepare to meet it as there is no doubt but that it will be amongst us in the spring. Some talk of running from it, but we think that the best way to meet it is to neither dread nor run from it but to prepare and use all persuasions against it. It is true that no one can tell but that himself

THE ROPE WALK

⟳   Hemp was one of Saline County's most profitable crops, and Arrow Rock was one of the towns in the Boonslick that had a "rope walk" to process the crop. The cultivation of hemp required year-around work and was dependent on slave labor. (State Historical Society of Missouri, Columbia)

may be the first victim to its dread ravages but if we use caution
we will at least stand a chance.

Cholera did strike the community. Reverend Gary Hickman, director of Lebanon Female Academy in Arrow Rock, lost his wife and son
to cholera in June 1849. Hickman was shaken by the tragedy but continued at the school for a time. In his 1853 pamphlet, "A Defense,"
he included a student's letters to an aunt. One, dated December 8,
1849, explains: "I am well pleased with this school. Mr. Hickman has
from 40 to 50 scholars. . . . I am studying grammar, philosophy, arith-
metic, reading and writing, modern history, and expect to com-
mence the study of chemistry after Christmas. . . . Mr. Hickman
makes us go to church every Sunday." Early the next year the student
wrote, "Mr. Hickman has taken a fool's fit. He is going to break up
school in 2 months. I do not know for certain his intentions, but
sometimes he talks of going to Lexington to teach school but I think
his intentions are to go to California."

Cholera claimed fifty lives in the county in 1850. Glen Hardeman
resumed his medical practice at Arrow Rock after his eventful, but
financially unsuccessful, trip to California. His slaves had continued
to work the farm, producing corn and hemp during his absence.
Hemp had been Missouri's first major cash crop and was still important. Saline County was the state's largest producer, and exports
were shipped from either Arrow Rock or Miami. Arrow Rock, along
with Rocheport and Glasgow, had a warehouse for storing hemp and
a rope walk for processing it. The hemp was sent to St. Louis, where
it sold for $160 per ton. From this was deducted freight costs of $10
per ton, insurance, storage, and sales commission, still leaving a
good profit. The wharf and docks on the Arrow Rock riverfront
stayed busy.

Duke Paul of Wuerttemberg made his third trip up the Missouri
River in 1851. Escaping European creditors, he had decided to
attend the Indian Treaty Council at Fort Laramie, and according to
excerpts from his diary of the trip, published in 1998 by Prince Hans
von Saxon-Altenburg and Robert L. Dyer, it proved the most hazardous of the expeditions he undertook. Accompanied by a young
German emigrant from Saxony and a German writer of western sto-

ries, Balduin Moellhausen, Duke Paul left St. Louis on August 21 on the *Pocahontas*. On August 23, the boat traveled from the mouth of the Osage to Arrow Rock. "There was not a breath of air. In the night the boat toiled several hours in the shoals in the vicinity of the Prairie [Pierre] de la Fleche above Boonville, where we stopped for half an hour at 9 o'clock." The duke was consulting his 1823 diary, so he must have remembered his earlier trials with his one-horse cart and young driver.

On an 1850 trip to California across Texas from New Orleans, Paul had met Johann Sutter and in a July 4 "parade to the California gold fields had ridden in the carriage with Sutter and the governor." Visiting Sutter's "New Switzerland," he noted that "one of these Snakes . . . a fine young lad, quite intelligent . . . reminded me strangely and with a certain sadness of B. Charbonneau, who had followed me in 1823 to Europe." After Charbonneau's return from his years in Europe with Duke Paul in 1829, many travelers wrote admiringly of him. One described him as "a gentleman of superior information . . . [who] had acquired a classic education and could converse quite fluently in German, Spanish, French, and English." When asked once why he lived in the wilderness, he replied, perhaps much as Duke Paul would have done, that he needed "to range the hills" and "could not be satisfied with the description of things [however] beautiful the style." In 1847, after U.S. forces took California, his abilities and services were recognized with an appointment as Alcade, or justice of the peace, at the mission in San Luis Rey. His duty was to "help take protective custody of the Indians" at the mission and see that they did not live an "idle, shiftless life." He resigned after less than a year, accused of supporting an insurrection, according to W. Dale Nelson, and "saying his Indian blood made it impossible for him to be impartial." He spent the rest of his life in the West, where his memory lived on among his mother's people. Carolyn Foreman wrote of a legend among the Shoshone of a youth who was educated "beyond the Great Ocean" and had told of "great houses on the water and people who wore wooden shoes."

On Duke Paul's return from the 1851 trip, "exhausted and emaciated," he reached Marshall on December 7 and after a detour "over a wretched road" arrived in Arrow Rock.

I have long been acquainted with its landing place due to my earlier journey. It is a flourishing little town and like the majority of places on the west bank is growing more rapidly than those on the northeastern bank. The Big La Mine River, which we crossed on a ferryboat, delayed us somewhat. We stopped at noon for only twenty minutes at the comfortably furnished home of a farmer, where we ate a good meal. The friendly man had a large family and handsome children.

The area had changed since 1823, when the "poor but good hearted" ferryman at the big Arrow Rock could only offer the duke "some old milk which had almost turned to cheese and some dried-out cornbread."

In the late 1840s the Grand Lodge of the State Independent Order of Odd Fellows organized in Arrow Rock. This organization was for working-class men and offered social activities, aid in finding work, and help for a member's family at a time of illness or death. New members had to be voted in, with members casting their votes using marbles. A white marble signified a yes vote, a black marble a no vote. The applicant for membership who was not accepted was said to have been "blackballed." George Caleb Bingham became a member of the Odd Fellows lodge, an indication of the kinship he felt with the working-class men of the day.

Workingmen, mostly trappers, boatmen, and settlers, peopled Bingham's work leading up to his 1851 painting *Daniel Boone Escorting Settlers through the Cumberland Gap,* showing frontiersmen with a group, including women and children, moving westward. Bingham dedicated the painting to his mother, who died that year and was buried in the Arrow Rock Cemetery. *The County Election,* 1851–1852, for which Arrow Rock residents posed, seems to reflect Bingham's feelings about the 1846 election, which the legislature had settled in favor of his opponent, Darwin Sappington. Bingham wanted the painting to express his conviction that the will of the people, not the will of the legislature, should be uppermost. He arranged to sell engravings of the painting, and he painted a second copy to show to prospective buyers.

In 1853, John Sappington decided to divide his property among his numerous heirs. But first he established the Sappington School Fund, which was to be used to educate the needy children of Saline County. He also gave nearly two acres of land one-quarter mile south of the Sappington Cemetery to Emanuel Banks, a longtime slave, to be used as a cemetery "for Negroes." He then allowed his heirs to bargain among themselves for the property each wanted, but according to Christopher Phillips, he stipulated that the portion of the pill business allotted to his Pearson grandchildren should come from Claiborne Fox Jackson's portion of the business, sending "a clear message to Jackson that he would not benefit from his marriage of convenience at his step children's expense." Jackson bargained with other heirs for working-age slaves and then bought the home place, Pilot Hickory, from the others, eventually renaming it Fox Castle. Eliza Jackson took care of her father for the next three years. Sappington entertained children and some adults by having a lead coffin made and stored under his bed. When he died in 1856, at age eighty-one, he was buried in that lead coffin next to his wife in the Sappington Cemetery.

During the 1850s, migration west continued. Hungarian immigrant John Xantus, whose boat got stuck in a sandbar at Arrow Rock during the winter of 1852–1853, observed that "Americans must like to travel." It seemed to him that "nine-tenths of the population was on the move all the time, pushing westward as the country became more settled."

By this time Arrow Rock had become a commercial distribution center for Cooper, Pettis, and Saline counties, with the river serving as the highway. That was to change as railroads began to come west. By 1855 the Pacific Line reached from St. Louis to Jefferson City. Saline County residents were willing to put up the funds to have access to a railroad, but prominent Pettis County citizens lobbied energetically for it, and the Pacific Railroad chose to go through the center of the state when it extended the line to Kansas City a decade later.

The first state fair had been held in 1853 in Boonville, and in 1856 an agricultural association was organized in Saline County, with former governor Marmaduke as president and future governor Jackson as a member. That same year Joshua L. Tracy, who had sold his boarding school in Boonville, moved to Arrow Rock and reorganized the girls' school, naming it the Arrow Rock Female Academy. Boarding pupils lived in a frame building near the tavern, which had originally been built as a log house.

On the national scene, John C. Frémont, by then settled in California and acclaimed as the "Pathfinder," accepted the nomination of the Republican party for president. George Bingham, although on his way to Europe in the summer of 1856, reportedly supported him, but Frémont's father-in-law, Thomas Hart Benton, did not. He favored Democratic party candidate James Buchanan, who believed the federal government had no right to interfere with slave states. Buchanan won the election.

In 1857 the widow and family of Louis Eversmann, a prominent German immigrant who had first settled near St. Louis, moved to Saline County. Stuart Voss observed that central Missouri, settled soon after the areas along the Mississippi River, would become "the challenged, not the challenger," in the "struggle for dominance and growth among the various sections of the state that took place during the next sixty-five years." Since the 1830s, a challenge to the "culturally southern enclave of the Boonslick" had been growing south of the Missouri River and west of St. Louis. Thousands of German immigrants developed villages, towns, farms, and businesses in what became known as the Missouri Rhineland. In 1824 Gottfried Duden, a German lawyer concerned about overpopulation and poverty in his homeland, had settled on a farm on Lake Creek west of St. Louis. Eversmann, an agricultural economist, accompanied Duden on his mission and bought a farm adjoining Duden's Hill. For the next three years, Duden recorded observations about life in Missouri, where he saw endless opportunities for his impoverished countrymen in the fertile land, low taxation, and need for services and products. When he returned to Germany, he published his *Report of a Journey to the Western States of America, and a Stay along the Missouri West of St. Louis*.

Historians consider Duden's book one of the most successful in encouraging immigration to America from German-speaking areas of central Europe. His vision of a "Little Germany" in the West appealed to well-educated revolutionaries, teachers, and romantics as well as the poor and unemployed, and a flood of German immigration to Missouri began in the 1830s that was to rival the "swarms" of emigrants from the South of which Sibley had spoken two decades earlier. The failed revolution of 1830 in Germany led to the development of several "emigration societies," and the 1848 revolution brought many refugee "forty-eighters." German settlements soon stretched along the Missouri from St. Louis to Jefferson City and as far west as Pettis and Lafayette counties. The majority of the German immigrants had left their homes to escape oppressive rulers, and many were outspoken in their opposition to slavery. Their presence was to have a profound influence on Missouri as the tension between North and South intensified.

Although most Germans opposed slavery, some became slave owners, among them Eversmann. Another German immigrant who came to Missouri a decade later, Gert Göbel, wrote, "Eversmann . . . whom I knew very well, became Americanized very quickly. He married an American from a very good family and very soon he became one of the first German slave holders." Few Germans followed his example, and Göbel said, "He was very wealthy but not very popular with his country men. . . . He sold his land on Lake Creek and planned to move to Saline County where he hoped to find more congenial company among the rich slaveholders there." Eversmann bought a farm north of Arrow Rock but died before he could move there. His family went on to Saline County and made their home there.

As the end of the 1850s approached, warehouses located on the Arrow Rock levee and businesses lining Main Street continued to thrive. The March 19, 1858, *Marshall Democrat* reported: "Drays, carts, and wagons are constantly traversing the streets between the steamboat landing and the business portion of the town, carrying hemp and other products of the farm for shipment, and returning with lumber, groceries, and other products for the county." As another indicator of the town's prosperity, the newspaper mentioned that the sidewalk on the north side of Main was widened to sixteen feet and on the south side to six feet, and that "stone gutters were cut and laid by slave labor, with each stone being laid two to three feet under the ground." There was also an article and many ads announcing that the cash system was in effect. Perhaps business owners were doubtful about the area's economic future or the money system since war seemed imminent.

But the town was booming. The activity at the river's edge continued even though there was no access from Main Street. The grade was too steep, and Burton Godsey's project was officially abandoned in 1858. Only a narrow gulch remained as a reminder of the high hopes of Arrow Rock businessmen. By 1858, sixty steamboats ran regularly on the Missouri River, with thirty to forty more called into use as necessary. Standing on the landing, observers might see as many as six boats at the dock. W. F. Johnson, in *History of Cooper County, Missouri,* writes that "during the boating season, from March to November, at no time was a boat not in sight." The boats were trim and fast, with two tall smokestacks that usually had ornamental tops. They hauled up to seven hundred tons of freight and perhaps four hundred passengers. Many residents enjoyed watching the steamboats arrive, but the Baptist Church, established in 1859, which met near Godsey's diggings, reportedly held meetings at about the time boats docked to keep their members from mixing with the travelers. Matthew Hall, whose home was also located near Godsey's diggings, moved his family to his farm to get his sons away from the "evil influence" of a port.

Residents organized other forms of entertainment, including a literary and debating club, which presented a play over Will H. Wood's store. The large hall featured "an elevated stage, drop curtain, and proscenium." Visiting lecturers sometimes came through, and the Levi J. North Circus came to town. Elbert G. Bowen wrote in *Theatrical Entertainments in Missouri before the Civil War* that "an assortment of singers, dancers, comedians, magicians, ventriloquists, and readers," toured the "hinterlands" of Missouri in the 1840s and 1850s. In 1845 the Great Philadelphia Zoological Garden advertised its itinerary through the middle of the state: Richmond, Liberty, Platte City, Westport, Independence, Wellington, Lexington, Arrow Rock, Boonville, and Palmyra. The Philadelphia show was one of the first of several menageries to reach the area before the war. "During the 1850s Missourians living near either the Mississippi or the Missouri rivers could see at least one circus each summer, and in several seasons they could take their pick of several sawdust shows." Wagon shows traveled up the Missouri River on the north side as far west as St. Joseph and then down the south side of the river on the return trip.

In 1857 a young single woman, Martha Wood, traveled from Virginia to Arrow Rock with her sister and brother-in-law, "Brother Cobb," and their children. Excerpts from her diary were published in *Hardship and Hope: Missouri Women Writing about Their Lives, 1820–1920*, edited by Carla Waal and Barbara Korner. The family left their home in Augusta County on March 17, 1857: "This day will ever be memorable as . . . the most painful of my life. The one on which I left my native country in the Old Dominion for a home in the far west," Martha wrote. Traveling overland by wagon, they crossed the Mississippi River into Mississippi County, Missouri, on April 22 and reached Saline County in early May. On May 9, Martha wrote: "Last evening and night were by far the most trying of my life; the roads were the worst I ever saw." The "Jersey wagon" had broken down, they had run out of provisions for the horses and were almost without food for themselves, and "the greatest of all our troubles was we heard late in the evening that our cousin had failed to rent us a home."

They were forced to camp out, but "a kind gentleman from Virginia" lived nearby and sent them corn and meal so that they "made out." By June 13 they had contacted many of their relatives in the area and their "cousin David B. Wood" had persuaded a bachelor friend to move in with him and let them have his house. Martha reported that family and neighbors had been generous with helping them get settled: "Our Uncle Milton offered land to cultivate free which was accepted very thankfully. . . . We had milk and butter given us. Our chickens were furnished to raise from, our ice is just given to us when we send to get it. New fresh meat, fresh fish, and many little varieties too tedious to mention are sent us" Although they had been dissatisfied with the area at first, and were still not perfectly satisfied, they liked it better. "The want of church privileges is our greatest cross," Martha wrote. On July 4 Martha attended the celebration of "glorious liberty in this state," at which Dr. Durrett, a Virginian boarding with Thomas Cobb in Arrow Rock, read the Declaration of Independence, and J. B. Price offered an oration "suitable to the occasion." She does not mention if any slaves were present for the Independence Day celebration of "glorious liberty."

Early in 1859 Thomas Cobb prepared to take over the Arrow Rock hotel and according to the *Marshall Democrat* "friend Cobb [was] hunting up new feathers and bed quilts to re-clothe it." That winter Martha's mother visited her daughters in Arrow Rock, and Martha accompanied her on the return trip to Virginia.

The slavery question increasingly dominated the thoughts and actions of Arrow Rock residents. Missourians were having to choose sides in the civil strife which plagued the area. In Saline County slavery had brought prosperity. The economy was largely based on slave labor, and slaves were valuable property with considerable money invested in them. A seventeen-year-old male would typically cost $1,300, a thirty-six-year-old male, $1,200, and a thirteen-year-old, $950. Most Saline County residents could not imagine a society without slaves. Though slave owners were in the minority, many other residents who did business with slaveholders were dependent on slavery for their financial survival, and stories of runaways caused great concern.

One of the most widely publicized escapes of a slave from Missouri had occurred in 1853, when Jack Burton ran away and disappeared into Canada. Jack had grown up in the household of Moses Burton, who had sold the boy's mother when Jack was seven. Slaves could not legally marry, but Jack had married Maria Tomlin, a slave in Fayette, by "slave custom." When he visited her, he often returned to the Burton farm late for work, and Moses Burton sold him to Colonel Reuben McDaniel of Saline County. A few months later, Jack fled the McDaniel farm. He stopped to see Maria, and north of Fayette, farmer Seneca Digges saw him and became suspicious. Digges ordered his slaves to catch him. As he ran, Jack suddenly came face to face with Digges and stabbed him, inflicting a fatal wound. The case became nationally known. The continuing unrest among the slaves caused slave owners to tighten already strict rules. The crime of one slave incited harsh action against him and others awaiting trial; a mob killed three slaves near the Saline County Courthouse. One was burned at the stake, and the others were hanged. Russell Hicks, the sixth district's circuit judge, who presided at the trial, was so shocked by the contempt people showed for the law that he refused to ever hold court in Saline County again.

Many Missourians were determined to see Kansas Territory enter the Union as a slave state. Otherwise, they feared that more slaves would be tempted to run, hoping to reach the state line and cross to freedom. To help the vote go their way, a number of Saline County men chose to be "Kansans" on voting day, making the trip to Kansas to vote illegally in territorial elections. Among them was Claiborne Fox Jackson, who was becoming one of the largest slaveholders in the state. Although George Caleb Bingham had ties to the South and had owned slaves until 1856, he aligned himself with the Republican party, which was committed to keeping slavery out of the territories, especially Kansas.

In 1859, despite concerns about war over the issue of slavery, entrepreneurs who planned to open a furniture shop, a dry goods store, and a grocery store built a three-story brick building in town; the Arrow Rock branch of the Bank of Missouri opened, and the *Saline County Herald* moved its presses from Marshall to Arrow Rock. Jay Potter became the telegraph operator when the lines, strung on trees, put Arrow Rock in contact with the world. The town's population was nearing 1,000.

Of great local interest that year was the possibility of a visit by now-famous artist George Caleb Bingham. The painter had married Eliza Thomas of Columbia in 1849 and in 1856 had gone with her and his daughter Clara to Europe to carry out a commission from the legislature to paint portraits of George Washington and Thomas Jefferson for the state capitol. When the paintings were completed, he personally accompanied them to Missouri, leaving his family in Germany. The December 9, 1858, *Weekly Democrat* of Marshall ran a paragraph from the *Columbia Statesman* announcing Bingham's expected return, then added its commentary:

> Mr. Geo. C. Bingham of this place, the distinguished "Missouri Artist," is daily expected at home from a long professional tour in Europe, during which he completed full length portraits of Washington and Jefferson for the State. These are to be suspended in the Capitol at Jefferson City, and it is said are master pieces of art, securing immortal fame to the artist.
>
> Mr. Bingham is, we believe, a native of this county, and repre-

sented it one term in the Legislature several years ago. The portraits in his painting of the County Election are many of them if not all from the faces of some of our worthiest citizens, and no one acquainted with the originals would fail to recognize them in the picture.

Mr. b's relatives still reside in Saline county.

On February 4, 1859, the *Weekly Democrat* ran an article, quoting the *Marshall Herald.*

> Wednesday's *Herald* has the following: We understand that this gentleman, who has earned a world wide reputation as an artist, who has been a long time absent in Europe, is now in Jefferson City, and expects soon to visit Saline county, his former home, and the scene of his early triumphs. We think the citizens of Saline county should receive him with some public expression of regard, not as a politician, but as a great man, a fellow-citizen, and one of the most distinguished artists of the age.

Interestingly, the *Herald's* editor encouraged Arrow Rock readers to support Bingham as an artist and "not as a politician," because, of course, Bingham's pro-union politics were not popular in Saline County. Although Bingham was a hometown success, residents who had watched him grow up and even posed for his portraits and genre paintings needed encouragement to welcome him. Historians cannot document that he visited in 1859, but Bingham did return to Arrow Rock in 1873 and was readily welcomed at that time.

Missouri's artist returned to Europe in 1859 with new commissions from the state legislature to paint portraits of Henry Clay and Andrew Jackson. Perhaps he chose to go to Europe to stay focused on his work since the political situation in the U.S., and certainly in Missouri, had become so complicated. Most people were not simply northerner or southerner, abolitionist or pro-slavery, pro-union or secessionist. Personal views of humanity, the economy, the necessity for unity, political leaders, the past, and concerns for the future complicated the issue. Bingham would eventually be caught up again in the political turmoil that shook his hometown, still a center of commerce and political influence. His talents and accomplishments were not limited to the visual arts, as the 1881 *History of Saline County, Missouri* states, in discussing the contradictions in his character.

> General Bingham was a very able and caustic writer as well as a gifted artist, and this faculty was frequently exhibited in controversies with other public men in Missouri. . . . General Bingham was the soul of honor, upright, liberal, gentle and true in all his relations, a companion whose society never wearied his friends, and whom they loved with constantly increasing affection, a member of the Baptist church, and an exemplary Christian.

Bingham had been involved in politics since the age of eighteen, when he attended the meeting in Saline County to discuss organizing a town on the bluff across from the big Arrow Rock, but for him, at this time, it must have seemed wiser to be *from* Arrow Rock than to be *in* Arrow Rock.

Chapter 6

A Place to *Be*,
Then a Place to Be *From*
1860–1887

In 1860, Arrow Rock had 1,000 residents. Saline County was now home to 9,800 white settlers and 4,886 slaves. The older and more established farms in the county were in the Arrow Rock area, which remained a center for political and social gatherings, medicine, shipping, and trade. *The Missouri State Gazetteer* for 1860 listed more than a hundred businesses, institutions, and organizations in the village, which bustled with builders, photographers, physicians, fishermen, laborers, ferrymen, boatmen, preachers, a liveryman, a mail contractor, a blacksmith, a woodworker, a wagonmaker, a miller, a tinner, a wool carder, a plasterer, a painter, a gunsmith, a shoemaker, a newspaper editor and a magistrate. Also serving the community were warehouses and stores—grocery, farm implement, furniture, hardware, boots and shoes, jewelry, millinery, and books. Henry S. Wilhelm, who had come to the village in 1836 to open a tailor shop, served as postmaster and mayor of Arrow Rock in the early 1860s.

Stuart Voss wrote, "Of all the central Missouri towns, Arrow Rock best characterized the strong Upper South tradition under the leadership of the gentry class" in the years before the war. Families lived on their large landholdings near the village, contributing to its prosperity by patronizing the businesses and using the services. Years later, Senator George G. Vest of Pettis County recalled visiting and dining at the Marmaduke farm near Arrow Rock on the eve of the war in 1860. It was, he remembered, "an event couched in the true Virginia style of cordial hospitality, good food and drink, and spirit-

93

Claiborne Fox Jackson, Missouri's fifteenth governor, fled the state during the Civil War and set up a state government in exile in Texas. (State Historical Society of Missouri, Columbia)

ed discussions of political and social issues." Arrow Rock would send two more men from its "gentry" class to the Missouri governor's office. The first would flee the state and set up a Missouri government in exile. The second would serve honorably and die in office.

Missouri had its largest hemp crop in 1860, and Saline County was the largest producer that year. While the slave owners enjoyed "spirited discussion of political and social issues," slaves labored over the hemp and other crops, and many must have thought of escape. The *Marshall Democrat* reported that between 1858 and 1859 twelve slaves in Saline County had run away. In December 1858 abolitionist John Brown had crossed from Kansas Territory into Missouri and led eleven slaves to Chicago. From there they traveled to Canada. Jack Burton, whose escape in 1853 had been widely publicized, was arrested in 1860 in Canada, where he had taken the name John Anderson. His trial attracted attention throughout the United States and abroad.

Witnesses to the stabbing of Seneca Digges and others went to Canada to testify, including Digges's sons, Thomas and Benjamin. Thomas had not seen the stabbing, and Benjamin, who had been only eight at the time could only say "the prisoner is about the color and size of the man, but I would not swear he is the man." The only witness who had known Jack Burton was Phil, one of Digges's slaves, and Missouri officials had taken a statement from him, but they did not send him to Canada. Anderson was convicted, but after a long appeal and argument about whether Digges had the authority under Canadian law to stop him, he was freed. In 1861 Canada sent the one-time Saline County slave to England, where he lectured and attended school. His British sponsors then decided he should go to Liberia, where the American Colonization Society had established a home for freed slaves, a decision he accepted unenthusiastically. Records show that Anderson boarded a ship for Liberia, but researchers have found no proof that he ever lived there.

During the next thirty years, Arrow Rock suffered under increasing tension, a savage war, and years of an uneasy peace. Union soldiers, Confederate soldiers, and bushwhackers came and went. What historian David Dary called "the slow death of the Santa Fe Trail" and the development of the railroad through neighboring Pettis County had their effect. Disease, fire, shipwrecks, drought, and grasshoppers also took their toll. Technology made farm operations and household duties possible with fewer helpers, and both black and white residents had to move away to find jobs.

Disappointment and heartache came early for Martha Wood and her sister's family. In March 1860 Martha returned to Arrow Rock from Virginia, taking the *Spread Eagle* steamboat up the Missouri River. She had learned that three of her sister's children had died, two nieces and a nephew, ranging in age from seven to sixteen. In spite of her grief, her trip upriver on the *Spread Eagle* had begun pleasantly enough. The captain, kind and obliging, had "asked permission to introduce several gentlemen to us, who proved to be very entertaining. 2 were sweet performers on guitar and fine singers, another a comic singer. Others, including my escort, were entertaining in conversation so we had a delightful evening." The next day, however, the only other unmarried lady got off. "Even the Capt. told me he was sorry for me for he said he had some hard customers on board." The reality of life in the Boonslick set in.

Martha found her sister, "who [had] been on the very verge of Eternity" recovering, but a few days later another nephew died. On April 14, she had a pleasant ride in the country with "our kind Dr. P.," but two days later she was "deeply depressed in spirits. . . . Our friends seem very distant." Martha's diary ended in 1860. When her brother-in-law, Thomas Cobb, left the Arrow Rock hotel in 1861, the diary was left behind, and researchers have found no further information about Martha.

Businessmen in Arrow Rock were interested in keeping the economy growing and hoped that war would not come. Many store owners depended on eastern markets for the goods needed by settlers, and the business community generally favored the North. The disagreement over slavery intensified with the question of whether to expand slavery into the western states, and that was not the only issue being debated. The temperance movement grew in Missouri as new immigrant groups established communities throughout the state, bringing their customs with them. In 1860 the largest foreign-born group in Saline County was German, and both Boonville and Lexington drew significant numbers of German immigrants. Although many were "substantial farmers and enterprising merchants and mechanics," Douglas Hurt reports that some residents expressed apprehension "because they came from Germany . . . and did not understand local customs or the language." German organizations often held plays and other events on Sundays. The depth of the Anglo-American disapproval of these practices was expressed in the outburst of a legislator when the Turner Society of Lexington applied for incorporation from the state senate. A Senator Thompson announced that he intended to vote against the bill, which he said "was intended to incorporate a set of infidel Dutch, who did not believe either in heaven, hell or the devil." He added that he "was surprised that such a bill would come from such a quarter. He was informed that there was much more than gymnastics to it."

Later, Charles D. Drake, speaking on behalf of a "Bill to Prevent Certain Practices on Sunday" admitted that he had never seen any of the performances and would not have understood them if he had since they were all in German, but it was a "matter of public notoriety" that they offended "all our ideas of propriety and morality." It was also well known that Germans had brought their love of beer and wine to the Boonslick and resisted temperance efforts to ban their festivities. Robert Dyer reports that feelings ran so high in Boonville, Sheriff B. B. Benedict stopped an itinerant temperance lecturer from speaking. He "considered the issue explosive enough that he banned any further gatherings." However, a Sons of Temperance group held a barbecue in Arrow Rock on July 4, 1860, and in 1861, the Sons of Temperance of Missouri held their semiannual meeting there.

Temperance faded in importance once the possibility of secession from the United States became the preelection issue that no one could avoid. Democratic support for presidential candidates was split three ways: Senator Stephen A. Douglas, supported by northern Democrats, did not own slaves, but he believed in the rights of states to decide for themselves whether slavery should be permitted. Southerner John C. Breckenridge represented the South's belief that slavery was a positive and necessary system and that a state had the right to withdraw, or secede, from the Union to perpetuate it. The Constitutional Union party, made up of former Whig party members, urged national unity and supported John Bell. The Republican candidate, Abraham Lincoln, had said, paraphrasing St. Matthew, that a nation half-slave and half-free could not endure. Claiborne Fox Jackson, who had won the Democratic nomination for governor of Missouri, supported Douglas for president, to the dismay of many in the Boonslick. Jackson won the election held in August 1860, however, with support from voters in St. Louis.

George Caleb Bingham backed the Republican candidate in the 1860 election, although he himself predicted war would result if Lincoln were elected. The artist again found himself aligned with Senator Thomas Hart Benton, whom he had opposed in his early years. Like Benton, he loved Missouri, but he loved the Union more. When Lincoln won the presidential election, South Carolina called a state convention, and in December it issued an ordinance dissolving the bonds between itself and the "United States of America."

Prominent citizens of Saline County sadly chose sides. Although from the South, former governor Meredith Miles Marmaduke supported the Union. His son, John Sappington Marmaduke, grandson of southern supporter John Sappington and nephew of Governor-elect Claiborne Fox Jackson, decided his loyalties lay with the South. The young Marmaduke had left home at midcentury for school in the East; he had attended both Yale and Harvard, graduated as a second lieutenant from West Point in 1856, and led troops on the frontier during the Mormon War. Glen Hardeman, a slaveholder descended from a long line of southerners, freed his slaves, and like Meredith Miles Marmaduke, chose to support the Union.

Bingham had returned from Europe early because of the death of his father-in-law, Robert S. Thomas, then living in Kansas City. Once home, Bingham completed the portraits of Henry Clay and Andrew Jackson the Missouri legislature had commissioned. As he presented them to the legislature, he quoted an earlier plea of Andrew Jackson, "Our Federal Union, it must be preserved," on the very day, January 7, 1861, that the secession issue was to be discussed by the legislature. As the debate intensified, Bingham continued to support the Union publicly.

Governor Claiborne Fox Jackson eventually tried to lead Missouri out of the Union. The largest slave owner in John Sappington's extended family, a longtime Democrat and state rights supporter, Jackson was outraged by federal attempts to force South Carolina to stay in the Union. When President Lincoln asked each state to send troops, Governor Jackson wrote Secretary of War Simon Cameron on April 17, 1861:

> Sir: -
> Your requisition is illegal, unconstitutional and revolutionary, in its object inhuman and diabolical.
> Not one man will Missouri furnish to carry on any such unholy crusade against her Southern sisters.
>
> Respectfully,
> C. F. Jackson

As Thomas L. Snead, Jackson's aide and secretary said, "He [Jackson] loved the Union, but not with the love with which he loved Missouri which had been his home for 40 years, nor as he loved the South, where he was born and where his kindred lived." Jackson not only refused Missouri troops to defend the Union's position, but he also began to raise state militia troops to ward off an attack by federal forces.

John Sappington Marmaduke, along with many other Saline County men, heeded Governor Jackson's call for the State Guard to defend Missouri against Brigadier General Nathaniel Lyon's volunteer pro-Union forces, which had advanced from St. Louis, taken Jefferson City, and continued west. The Battle of Boonville on June 17, 1861, was not a large battle, but as the second land battle of the Civil War, it had huge political ramifications. Hearing that federal troops were approaching Lexington from Kansas, General Sterling Price had moved to meet them. Marmaduke advised that the battle with Lyon's forces be postponed, but Jackson ordered him to proceed. Having been put in charge by his uncle, Marmaduke was largely blamed for the quick defeat of the untrained and poorly armed State Guards by the more experienced, well-armed volunteer troops, some of whom had fought in Germany. Howard W. Marshall, a native of what came to be known as "Little Dixie," believes Marmaduke was the victim of bad luck and poor planning by his superiors. The Battle of Boonville became known as the "Boonville Races," for the State Guard's speedy retreat and Governor Jackson's flight south in his carriage.

As a result of the battle, Missouri stayed in the Union under an appointed governor, Hamilton Gamble of Howard County, and Jackson and his family took their slaves and went to Texas. There Jackson set up a government in exile. He later joined the Confederates in Arkansas with plans to retake Missouri for the South, but he died in 1862 and was buried in Arkansas. His wife, Eliza, died two years later in Texas. Not until 1871 were their bodies moved to Sappington Cemetery near Arrow Rock.

The *Saline County Herald* ceased to publish when George Allen, editor and publisher, and his son joined the Confederate Army. Even Governor Gamble believed, "If Missourians listened to their hearts they would go with the South; if to their minds, with the North." He listened to his mind as others did. Glen Hardeman was one of many who had wished to stay neutral. In Missouri that was

John Sappington Marmaduke, son of Meredith
Miles Marmaduke, fought for the Confederacy during the Civil War but still became Missouri's twenty-
fifth governor. He died in office in 1887. (State
Historical Society of Missouri, Columbia)

impossible. When forced to choose, Hardeman stayed loyal to the
Union and began to report those who were not to authorities. Bushwhackers threatened him at gunpoint, but according to reports, did
not shoot because his wife, Permelia, threw herself in front of him.
Unsafe at home in Missouri, Hardeman then volunteered as a sur-
geon in the Union Army. Some men fled to Canada, some to California, and others to Northern states, but before the war's end, more
than 60 percent of Missouri's men of military age, higher than that
of any other state, went to war on one side or the other.

John Sappington Marmaduke, like others in Saline County, had found it hard to choose between the Union and the Confederacy, but five days after the firing on Fort Sumter, he resigned his U.S. Army commission. After the disaster at Boonville, he resigned from the State Guard and went to Virginia to join the Confederate Army. Receiving a commission as a lieutenant colonel, he fought in actions in Tennessee, Arkansas, and Missouri. He was wounded at Shiloh, and in Arkansas he mortally wounded another Confederate officer, General Lucian Walker, in a duel. General Sterling Price had ordered him to stay in his quarters instead of meeting Walker and had him arrested after Walker's death, but Marmaduke was never charged. Price needed him for a planned attempt to take Missouri for the Confederacy.

Marmaduke commanded a vanguard of Confederate forces in General Price's invasion of southeast Missouri in the fall of 1864. He led his troops through Pilot Knob to Hermann, a known Unionist stronghold. Hermann historians have told of a ruse the few older men remaining in the town used to try to hold Marmaduke's troops off until the town could be evacuated. Lookouts had warned of the approaching troops, and as the Confederates reached the edge of town, they were met with cannon fire, first from one hill and then another. Knowing all the young men were in the Union Army, Marmaduke thought he was engaged by enemy troops and sent out a scouting party. The scouts found one cannon, which the men too old for active army service had dragged from hill to hill to give the impression that Hermann was surrounded. The men then left town with the women and children. The Confederates pushed the cannon into the river. (It was retrieved after the war and now stands in front of the Hermann courthouse).

Marmaduke's troops camped on the property in Hermann adjoining George Husmann's winery. When they discovered the wine cellar, they opened all the barrels and let the wine run into the river. Price's army retreated westward the next day, and in an engagement at Westport, Marmaduke had two horses shot from under him. He survived, only to be captured as Price withdrew south, and he spent the rest of the war in prison in Massachusetts. He had been promoted to brigadier general after Shiloh and was promoted to major general while in prison.

George Caleb Bingham had enlisted in the Union Army as a private when the war began, but he had been named captain of Company C in Kansas City; he commanded the company at the Battle of Lexington in September 1861. Using wetted hemp bales as shields, the Confederates, led by Sterling Price, forced the Union to surrender after a three-day siege and a fierce battle. As more federal troops, commanded by Frémont, approached, Price led his troops to southwest Missouri to join Claiborne Jackson. Because he felt ill-suited for the military, Bingham asked to be named a consul abroad. Instead, he was appointed state treasurer, and while in Jefferson City he was commissioned to paint the portrait of General Nathaniel Lyon, who had died in the Battle of Wilson's Creek August 10, 1861. Bingham admired the general and was pleased to do Lyon's portrait, but he was not always as pleased with other Northern leaders as the war progressed.

At the convention of the Union Provisional Government of Missouri, held after Jackson had left the state, delegates formulated a loyalty oath, which was first required in 1861. Throughout and after the war, Missourians were required to swear allegiance both to the state and the federal constitutions, as well as avow not to aid the Confederacy, if they wanted to stay in business or hold any kind of office. Some residents of the Boonslick left the state to avoid signing the oath. John Scott, who had opened a "Cash and Barter" store in 1846 in Miami in Saline County, had to sign the oath and pay a bond in order to continue his business. His wife, Elvira, wrote an account after the war of her husband's troubles and her own during the occupation of Miami by a company of Union soldiers. Published in *Hardship and Hope* by Carla Waal and Barbara Korner, the diary reports encounters between the Scotts and their neighbors and Union officers and soldiers.

John Scott, whose partner was Reuben McDaniel, former owner of escaped slave Jack Burton, was sympathetic to the Confederacy, but he wanted to keep his business going. Elvira, as she admitted in her diary, "was very fond of talking," and she soon found talk could be dangerous. Although she and her daughter played the piano for the music-loving federal soldiers, she apparently could not hide her feelings, and in July 1862 she was served with a military notice informing her that a "Ladies place is to fulfill her household duties and not spread treason and excite men to rebellion." She was directed to report to the commanding officer every Friday morning until he was "fully convinced that you will behave yourself as a Lady ought." If she did not comply, according to the notice, her husband would be sent to the military prison in Marshall. Others had received the notice, as well, and the women decided that they would go together to the commanding officer. They asked so many questions and demanded so many explanations of the language in the notice and his definition of treason that in the end the lieutenant was glad to get rid of them. The Scotts eventually moved to St. Louis for the duration of the war, but Union soldiers remained in Miami. In 1864 John William Boone, "Blind Boone," Missouri's famous musician, who became a nationally known performer, was born there. His father was a Union soldier and his mother the camp cook.

Some Confederate sympathizers suffered far more than Elvira Scott. General Thomas Ewing, in response to William Quantrill's raid on Union supporters in Lawrence, Kansas, had taken prisoner the wives and sisters of Quantrill's guerrillas. Union troops had housed the women in George Caleb Bingham's Kansas City house, without his permission. The building collapsed in August 1863, killing many of the women, including the sister of "Bloody Bill" Anderson, and injuring others. Bingham was outraged. After he had turned his back on his Southern background and supported the North, Union troops had illegally seized his home to imprison Missouri citizens. There was talk that soldiers had damaged the building, perhaps purposely weakened it, then escaped, leaving the women to be injured or killed. Bingham's anger grew as he witnessed the effects of Ewing's infamous Order No. 11. The order, issued in August 1863, forced Missourians who lived along the border with Kansas, near Kansas City, from their homes, which were then looted and destroyed. Even those who had remained loyal to the North during the war were displaced.

During 1863, while little but war occupied the minds of most Missourians, Arrow Rock residents continued to receive visitors from around the world. An Englishman, Albert Richardson, published an account of his travels up the Missouri by wood-burning steamer, *Beyond the Mississippi*. His destination was Kansas City, but the steamer had to pass Arrow Rock. Other passengers on the boat included young men and married couples from the East seeking better opportunities, missionaries, nuns, medical students, gamblers, teachers, writers, and speculators. Upon reaching Kansas City, Richardson noted, "Once during low water, the trip took nine days. This trip to Kansas City from St. Louis had taken two days and we all thought it excellent time. The trains now accomplish it in the wonderful space of only 14 hours." While minds focused on war, technology was changing travel—another reason that life would never be the same, especially not in Arrow Rock.

No major battles occurred in Arrow Rock, but accidents and guerrilla actions were hard on the little town and its people. In 1864 sparks from the steamboat *Isabella* set fire to four warehouses along the Missouri River. In July of that year one hundred of Quantrill's guerrillas led by a Captain Yager attacked a Union garrison of twenty-five men, under the leadership of Lieutenant D. P. Woodruff, who were occupying a building in Arrow Rock.

According to *History of Saline County, Missouri,* the guerrillas set fire to buildings, including the garrison, forcing a Union retreat "and this they did under the cover of darkness, without the loss of a man," but they had to leave their horses behind. In the ensuing battle, several guerrillas, including Yager, were wounded.

Meredith Miles Marmaduke, who had served as eighth governor of Missouri, died in 1864 and was buried in Sappington Cemetery with Masonic honors. William Napton, a historian, wrote of him: "A man of earnest and purposeful life, he was one to be trusted and his integrity was never impeached nor his character blemished. His life was characterized by a constant endeavor to do the right as he understood the right and in his death the community and the state suffered a distinct loss."

In November of 1864 Abraham Lincoln was reelected president, and at his second inaugural on April 4, 1865, he appealed to the nation to put aside thoughts of vengeance: "With malice toward none; with charity for all . . . let us . . . . bind up the nation's wounds . . . do all which may achieve . . . a just and lasting peace." On April 2, General Robert E. Lee, his army battered and badly outnumbered, had evacuated Richmond. On April 9, he met General

Ulysses S. Grant at Appomattox Court House to discuss terms of surrender. The two men quickly came to terms: Lee's soldiers were paroled home, officers retained their sidearms, and soldiers could retain their private horses and mules. The Union Army issued 25,000 rations to the Confederates.

In his last public address on April 11, President Lincoln again pleaded for reconciliation. To retain the loyalty of the slaveholding border states, Lincoln had resisted the demands of the Radical Republicans to abolish slavery. In August 1861, when General John Frémont had issued a proclamation declaring that slaves of Missourians who took up arms against the U.S. were free, Lincoln modified his order to conform to existing law and relieved Frémont of his command as major general of the department of the West in St. Louis. Lincoln's Emancipation Proclamation of January 1, 1863, had declared that all slaves in areas still in rebellion were "then and forever free." It did not free slaves in Missouri, who had remained in bondage throughout the war.

However, in January 1865, three months before Lee's surrender, the Missouri State Constitutional Convention, meeting in St. Louis, enacted "An Ordinance Abolishing Slavery in Missouri." It was signed into law to take effect immediately, but most Missourians, slaves and slave owners alike, did not learn of it for some time. The war ended, and slaves were freed, but the turmoil continued in Saline County. The reconciliation that Lincoln had hoped for did not come easily.

In 1865, it was considered too dangerous for tax collector Benjamin H. Hawpe to travel the county alone to collect the revenue. On March 9, the court ordered taxpayers to meet him in Marshall. Glen Hardeman returned to Arrow Rock but was not welcomed by his former neighbors. He moved to eastern Missouri in 1866. After five years, he tried living in Saline County again, but again returned to his new home in the eastern part of the state. In *Along the Old Trail*, T. C. Rainey reported that when he came to town in 1865, "The war was just over, and returned soldiers from both armies were back home. There was no cordiality between them, particularly between those, on both sides, who had skirmished around without doing much fighting. The actual soldiers fraternized better."

In 1865 the well-known tavern owner Joseph Huston died. Will

Wood, a local man who had been a clerk, grocer, and steamboat businessman, started a grocery business. Bingham, after finishing his term as state treasurer and moving to Independence, began a painting in protest of Brigadier General Thomas Ewing's Order No. 11. Bingham was quoted as declaring, "With this painting I will make this order infamous." *Order No. 11* reminded the public of the terrors of civil war, and many believe the painting affected Ewing's political future. According to Napton's 1910 Saline County history, "[Ewing] never recovered from the reputation gained by Order No. Eleven . . . represented and perpetuated on canvas by the Missouri artist, Gen. George C. Bingham, who also fought on the Federal side, as did General Ewing."

In his *Missouri: A Bicentennial History,* Paul Nagel observed that, although the bulk of Missouri's slave population was concentrated in central Missouri, any resemblance of the area's society and economy to that of the southern plantation states was "more imagined than real." After the Civil War, however, its "citizens redoubled efforts to foster what were remembered as some of the qualities of Southern life. This meant . . . [segregation] between blacks and whites, upholding the conservative arm of the Democratic party, and preserving styles in architecture, cooking, sport, and recreation presumed to be part of the southern tradition. . . . For a significant and influential part of the population, preserving a landed aristocratic view was consoling and necessary." Historians have noted that the early settlers in the Boonslick considered themselves westerners. By the end of the Civil War many considered themselves southerners, so much so that eventually the Boonslick area came to be known as Little Dixie and to pride itself on its southern heritage.

Meanwhile, social events were again possible. The wedding of William B. Sappington Jr. and Jennie Brown in 1867 brought distinguished visitors to the area. Former Confederate Major General John S. Marmaduke was among the wedding guests. Following the wedding, fifty to sixty guests boarded a boat, which traveled to Miami, the port just beyond Arrow Rock. A German orchestra played during the entire trip, which took a day and two nights. Half the orchestra members slept while the other half played.

As white residents of Arrow Rock struggled to rebuild their lives after the war, freed slaves had reason to hope for a better future. The general assembly rescinded the old restrictions on education for black children in the spring of 1865, but it made no monetary provisions for schools that year. If the number of black children in an area exceeded twenty, school was to be kept open for a winter term equivalent to that provided white children, but lack of teachers, lack of funds, and apathy, if not hostility, on the part of local officials hindered efforts to establish schools for black children in many areas of the state.

In the late 1860s James Milton Turner traveled throughout Missouri to investigate conditions in black schools for the Freedmen's Bureau and the state superintendent of schools, Radical Republican Thomas A. Parker. Turner, who had been freed as a child, had attended secret St. Louis schools for black children and later Oberlin College in Ohio. In early November 1869, according to his biographer, Gary Kremer, he hired a buggy in Boonville and drove to Arrow Rock to investigate "an alleged fraud that resulted in insufficient funds to build a school for black children." The local board of education spokesman, Henry Wilhelm, seemed willing to do his best, an attitude Turner had not often found elsewhere. Wilhelm told Turner that because the board had not received the money due it, building a new school was not possible, but he offered instead to use "money belonging to white children to open a school in [a] colored church building now in the course of erection and run the same four months." Based on earlier experiences, Turner could not quite believe Wilhelm's promise and took steps to ensure that the children got the school.

Historian Lawrence O. Christensen quotes from Turner's letter to F. A. Seely of the Missouri Freedmen's Bureau.

> I called a meeting of colored people and made them promise to complete the house in 15 days. I think old man Wilhelm talks most too kind to be relied upon, and I shall ask Mr. Parker to send him a 20-day notice. . . I have told the colored people to tease old Man Wilhelm until he gives them a school that he may be rid of them.

 John Thomas Trigg taught in the Arrow Rock African American school from 1889 until the late 1920s. (Friends of Arrow Rock)

Turner told Seely he thought there would be a school in Arrow Rock in twenty to twenty-five days.

Trying to help themselves as best they could, former slaves came together to build schools in white communities and to establish all-black settlements or villages. Pennytown in Saline County, located a few miles from Arrow Rock, was founded in the 1870s. It got its name from Joseph Penny, who came to Saline County in the late 1860s and in 1871 brought eight acres of land from a white man, John Haggin, for $160. He sold plots to other blacks, and during the next few years others bought adjoining property. By 1879 the group of settlers owned almost sixty-four acres. There were other "historic black ham-

lets" in Saline County, according to historians Lynn Morrow and
Gary Kremer, but Pennytown became the largest and the most successful. During the next three decades these new pioneers were to
achieve a remarkable success.

Lodge and church events remained important parts of community life for both blacks and whites. The Independent Order of Odd
Fellows (IOOF) Lodge built a two-story hall in 1868. They rented
out the ground floor and met on the second floor of the building.
The Arrow Rock Masonic Lodge constructed a building the same
year. The Arrow Rock Church of Christ was built in 1871 on land
probably donated by John Sites, the gunsmith, and his wife. Sites
served as deacon and trustee, and the couple were active members
of the church. The Methodist Episcopal, later called ME South, which
had organized in 1831, worshipped in a frame building built in 1849.
The Cumberland Presbyterian, organized in 1853, met in a frame
building built in 1857. After the Baptists organized a congregation
in 1859, they built a frame church. African Americans worshipped
in their Methodist Church and Brown's Chapel, a Free Will Baptist
church built by freed slaves in 1869. However, growth of these con-
gregations was limited; population of the village was in decline.

The war and its aftermath had brought hardship and tragedy to
many Missourians, including those in Saline County. As quickly as
the "landed gentry" and the businessmen had achieved prosperity in
the decades prior to the Civil War, their means of making a living
disappeared during and after the war. Immigration west and traffic
on the Missouri River slowed, the market for hemp decreased dra-
matically, and farms and businesses lost the slave labor that had cre-
ated their prosperity. Stuart Voss found that "in general the towns in
the northwestern half of the region (Arrow Rock, Glasgow, Fayette,
Rocheport) suffered the most." Arrow Rock had been harassed by
"military rule, sudden arrests, and guerrilla raids," Voss wrote. Unfor-
tunately, lawlessness continued to plague the state, and Arrow Rock
was not exempt. Ruffians who had used the war as an excuse to rob
and plunder now continued to disregard the law. Citizens who did
not feel that they could trust local officials to protect them formed
a vigilante group known as the Honest Men's League and took the
law into their own hands. According to oral accounts, following a

☞ Brown's Chapel served as one of the first school buildings for black residents. According to the 1870 census, sixty-five students were attending the school in the fall of 1870. (Friends of Arrow Rock)

disastrous fire in 1873 that started in a saloon on Fourth Street and spread to Main Street, a mob lynched one or more of the young men accused of setting it. Attempting to exert some control, the city fathers paid to have a "one-man" jail constructed in 1873.

Nature and accidents also plagued the area during the 1870s. In the years following the war, grasshoppers had become an increasing problem for farmers. The state legislature offered to pay a dollar per bushel for grasshoppers in March of 1877; fifty cents in April, and twenty-five cents in May. They paid five dollars per bushel for grasshopper eggs any time. Accidents had no season. According to E. J. Melton, in a history of Cooper County, *Plow Boy II,* which burned at the Arrow Rock dock July 7, 1877, is one of the seven boats sunk into the river bottom near Arrow Rock.

The extension of railroads had a major effect on the postwar

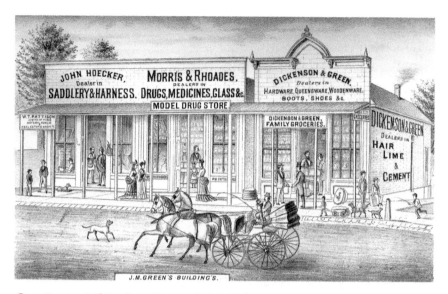

In the 1870s the effects of the Civil War were still being felt in the Boonslick, and Arrow Rock businesses were struggling to survive. According to Charles van Ravenswaay, the wide walkways in front of the stores were designed so that ladies in hoopskirts could pass one another. (*Saline County Atlas, 1876,* courtesy State Historical Society of Missouri, Columbia)

economy. George R. Smith, a member of the state legislature who had settled in Pettis County in the 1840s, lobbied the railroad to "follow the inland route across the prairie." A stagecoach ran from Arrow Rock to Marshall, and freight that came to the Arrow Rock dock was delivered by a wagon with three yoke of oxen, but as railroads extended west, wagons and boats lost out to railroad cars. As both the railroad and major roads cut through the center of the state, Arrow Rock was no longer on the route of travelers. By 1880, after sixty years of use by tradesmen and soldiers, the Santa Fe Trail, covering nine hundred miles between mid-Missouri and Mexico, was officially considered closed. Two- and three-story buildings on Main Street, the Santa Fe Trail, river traffic, large farming operations, the steamboat era, political power, and a famous artist in residence were fast becoming only memories to the remaining residents.

Fewer and fewer of Arrow Rock's sons returned to the now out-of-the-way village.

John Sappington Marmaduke never returned to Arrow Rock to live; after serving in the army, he tried a number of business ventures in St. Louis. With the war over, he encouraged Missourians by example, leadership, and legislation to forge ahead with the endless possibilities in the state for growth and progress. In January 1886 Marmaduke became Missouri's twenty-fifth governor, the sixth to occupy the new governor's mansion overlooking the Missouri River, which had been built in 1871. In one of the ironies of Missouri history, he followed Governor Thomas Crittenden, who had lived in Lexington before the war. A strong Unionist, reportedly one of twenty-seven men in Lexington who favored the Union, Crittenden had fought in the Battle of Shiloh, where Marmaduke was wounded, and in the Battle of Westport, where Marmaduke was captured.

As he anticipated becoming governor, Marmaduke, a bachelor, had planned that his mother, Lavinia, daughter of John Sappington and a widow for the last twenty-two years, would serve as hostess in the mansion. But his mother and two of his sisters were gravely ill on inauguration day. Marmaduke, his widowed niece, Lalla Marmaduke Nelson, and her young son moved into the mansion and prepared to entertain only a few friends and relatives that first evening. As he settled into the governor's mansion, Marmaduke must have thought of the two men from Arrow Rock who had served as governor before him. Twenty years earlier, Claiborne Fox Jackson, his uncle, had spent only a short time in Jefferson City in the 1834 wood-and-stone two-story governor's mansion, situated near the capitol. Still earlier, Marmaduke's father, Meredith Miles Marmaduke, moved into that same governor's home to serve out the term of Governor Reynolds. On the Confederate withdrawal from Hermann toward Westport, Marmaduke had reportedly stood on a hill overlooking Jefferson City and pointed to the capitol, saying, "Gentlemen, you see that capitol yonder. I will live to occupy it as governor of the state of Missouri."

In her history of the governor's mansion, *If Walls Could Talk*, former first lady of Missouri Jean Carnahan quoted from a story in the *Kansas City Star* on Marmaduke: "He was not a lawyer. He was not a merchant. He was not a farmer. He was not a business man. He was

Ⓢ   Robert Banks was born a slave. This photograph
was made around 1915 in front of the old tavern.
(Missouri Department of Natural Resources)

not a public speaker—at best a poor one. He was not a writer, nor a
great editor. He was a military man out of a job." Nevertheless, John
Sappington Marmaduke, who had held several jobs after the war,
including that of editor of an agricultural journal, proved to be a
good and compassionate governor.

Marmaduke was described as having "fervor yet common sense."
He had the mansion updated and displayed George Caleb Bingham's
paintings, including a portrait of his father. He had the capitol heat-
ing system updated, passed legislation governing railroads, increased
the emphasis on funding for schools, and held parties for children.

The wedding of Marmaduke's niece helped brighten the otherwise difficult first year of his term after the deaths of his mother and two sisters. A second niece, Iola Harwood, daughter of the governor's late sister, then became hostess.

On Christmas Day 1887, Marmaduke wrote the Colored State Teachers' Association of Missouri that he would not be able to attend their meeting. He assured them that he, and the Democratic party, were in favor of education for their people. He added, "As a former slave owner and the son and grandson of slave owners, I say frankly I am glad slavery is forever abolished in the United States. I do not think the way it was eradicated either right or necessary." He had made plans for the third annual children's Christmas party, but he became ill and died on the date set for the party, December 28, 1887. The state mourned the death of a governor who was greatly loved, and Lieutenant Governor Albert P. Morehouse, who had been a Union officer, served out Marmaduke's term.

Marmaduke's brother, Darwin, wrote that he had "died without money" because of his generosity. The newspapers had published a story about a woman who sent him a Confederate twenty-dollar bill he had used to pay her for providing him with a meal and caring for his horse during the war. He replaced it with U.S. currency but asked the newspaper not to print this fact, fearing he would be swamped with requests to cover Confederate bills he had handed out in Missouri.

Marmaduke was buried in the Woodlawn Cemetery in Jefferson City, and funds were raised in Jefferson City for a monument for his grave. The family planned to have the body of the governor taken to the Sappington Cemetery near Arrow Rock to be buried with his grandfather, John Sappington; his father, Meredith Miles Marmaduke; and his uncle, Claiborne Fox Jackson, but weather made the last trip to Arrow Rock impossible.

Travelers continued to visit and note Arrow Rock's past political and social prominence, but even in death, most sons and daughters did not return to their roots. Like the now world-famous artist George Caleb Bingham, who had died in Kansas City in 1876, residents, both black and white, moved on, perhaps mentioning, as the topic arose, that they were "*from* Arrow Rock."

Chapter 7

Sleepy Village
1888–1949

In the years following the Civil War, many residents of Arrow Rock had moved to larger towns to find work, but for the families of Ruth Wilson Banks, Dorothy Mosely Kruger, and Mary Rinne Stith, the sleepy village of Arrow Rock remained a good place to be.

Banks's extended family is in many ways typical of African American families after the war. Many former slaves stayed on the farms or worked and lived in the homes or businesses of their former owners. Farmers and farm wives needed help. Preparing food, making clothing, and cleaning took hours of time, and many African American women found work as domestic help. This was the situation for Callie Cooper, Ruth Banks's beloved grandmother. Ruth called her "mamma." "We loved her," Ruth said. "She stayed with white folks and took care of their chil'ren; she didn't stay in a home like we did. She stayed with white folks, cause we was slave chil'ren. My mamma belonged to the slave people." Ruth's parents, Frank and Betty Wilson, also continued to work in the Arrow Rock area, but they were free—free to assemble, move, marry, and learn to read and write.

By 1891, Arrow Rock was becoming something of a summer resort. "Every house in town is occupied and the courthouse is full of strangers who have come here to spend the hot weather. For [quiet], morality, and health our city is not excelled in all this country," reported the newpaper. Residents formed an Arrow Rock Library Society in July of 1891. Thirty-three subscribers paid $2.75

each, enough to buy 132 volumes of "miscellaneous works." "There can be no enterprise . . . where the principle of cooperation can be applied with greater advantage . . . than that of a library society," the editor commented.

By October summer visitors had gone, and the writer of "Local Matters" complained, "A person who could make an interesting local page in these times could make cheese out of rainwater." The towns-people could look forward to "one rare treat," however. The ladies of the Cumberland Presbyterian Church were planning a fund-rais-ing concert of "vocal and instrumental selections, tableaux, recita-tions, etc. This promises to be a rare treat as not only home talent will be employed, but elocutionists from elsewhere . . . are expected to attend."

The paper for February 19, 1892, carried political news: "Since Darwin Marmaduke's announcement as candidate for the Demo-cratic nomination for governor some newspapers find reason for opposing him on the ground that his father and brother were both honored with that office." Marmaduke reminded them, "My father was elected Lieut. Governor in November, 1840, for the term of four years. On the death of governor Reynolds, February 9th 1844, he became acting governor and served for the remainder of the term. . . . My brother, Jno. S. Marmaduke, was elected governor in 1884, and had served only three years at the time of his death." Darwin Marmaduke said, "If they were faithful public servants, I do not see why it should disbar me from aspiring to this honorable position." He did not mention the third governor from Arrow Rock, his uncle Claiborne Fox Jackson.

Like most mid-Missouri towns of any consequence, Arrow Rock had from time to time a weekly newspaper. The first, the *Saline County Herald,* was published by George Allen until 1861, when he and his son joined the Confederate Army. Allen was killed in the Battle of Wilson's Creek near Springfield. Except for the short-lived *Democratic Cable,* published from 1870 to 1871, no newspaper was published until 1881, when the *Arrow Rock Times* began publishing. It ceased publication in 1890, and the *Arrow Rock Enterprise* had a very brief run in 1891, but the *Arrow Rock Statesman* endured from 1893 until 1919. A second *Arrow Rock Times* followed, but it lasted only a year.

Cordell Tindall temporarily revived the *Arrow Rock Enterprise* in 1987, reprinting earlier articles.

While the whites of Arrow Rock were forming a library society and reading whatever local newspaper was in business, African Americans were building churches and lodges and establishing schools so that their children could learn to read.

The Baptist church, Brown's Chapel, probably served as the first schoolhouse. By 1880, sixty-five black students were attending school in Arrow Rock township, many of them young adults. In 1892, when a new school for white children was built, the salvaged bricks and lumber from the old building were used to build a school for black children. Some black children did not attend school. Ruth Banks Perry remembered that her mother said they didn't need education. Although her parents did not send their children to school, Ruth did have the opportunity to learn from others. Ruth's mother cared for the children of a farmer, whose wife took an interest in Ruth and her siblings. "This white woman . . . she learn us what we know. She said when you get up big you gonna have to know how to count money and write your name. If you know how to count money, can't nobody beat you out of nothin'. She taught us—that woman taught us." Ruth could not recall the name of the white woman who employed her mother and took an interest in her, but she remembered, "She gave me a sheep to raise. I was to raise the young sheep and sell them to make money to put in the bank. She started me out," Perry explained. "That was really nice."

In addition to the Baptist and Methodist churches, African Americans built four lodges in Arrow Rock. Each lodge had auxiliaries for women and for youth. These organizations served as a source of funds and aid for members in time of illness or death and provided a base for social life.

Black families now enjoyed a variety of activities, with church events as the core. As Ruth recalled of the years before her marriage, "Mamma fixed us up on Sundays for Sunday School and church and she'd go with us to Freewill Baptist—Brown's Chapel. They brought you up to go to church, and they let you go to dances, but it had to be one they could go with you and see that everything was turnin' out all right. They didn't turn the children loose. They went and seen

Ⓢ   The old tavern was a popular place for Sunday dinner in the 1930s.
(State Historical Society of Missouri, Columbia)

that everything was all right." Families also held dances in their
homes, and the black community gathered for social events that had
been denied them during slavery. Ruth said, "When me and Jake
[Banks] got married, Mamma had a big dinner and had a lot of people there. They had string music and we danced. We really had a
wonderful time and that was about the happiest day."

The town's fortunes rose and fell as the new century began. Early
in the 1900s, longtime leader of the Democratic party and Democratic presidential candidate William Jennings Bryan spoke from the
balcony of the house that William Price had built in Arrow Rock. Perhaps his speech gave residents a fleeting taste of the village's former
glory as a political center. But the residents had some rebuilding to
do. In 1901, a fire, started when a lamp tipped over in the drugstore,
destroyed all the buildings on the north side of Main Street.

By this time, only a few steamboats tied up at the dock, and opportunities for former farm workers continued to decline. The town was no longer a center for commerce, politics, or extravagant social gatherings, but new opportunities developed. People were beginning to recognize Arrow Rock's importance as a historic gathering place for Native Americans, hunters, explorers, traders, soldiers, and settlers. The Missouri Society of the Daughters of the American Revolution (DAR) joined in a national effort to place markers along the old trails from the East Coast to the West. The DAR encouraged members to pay particular attention to taverns that had served those traveling west. Because of its connection with the Santa Fe Trail, the Arrow Rock Tavern drew the attention of the DAR and its companion group, the Women's National Old Trails Association. In 1912, the DAR established a museum room in the tavern as "a means of teaching Missouri history to the passerby." The interest in interpreting Arrow Rock's history for visitors grew steadily during the next decades.

During the late nineteenth and early twentieth centuries, the residents of the all-black settlement of Pennytown, thirteen miles southwest of Arrow Rock, continued to build an economic, cultural, and social life for themselves. Lynn Morrow and Gary Kremer, writing in the 1990 Missouri *Folklore Society Journal,* described a utopian community. A study of the agricultural census of 1880 suggested to the historians that a division of labor and sharing of resources took place within the community.

> Of eleven landowners, three had some machinery, eight had a horse or two, six had milk cows (though only four produced butter), seven had swine, three raised wheat, seven raised corn, two raised tobacco, three raised Irish potatoes, three raised apple trees, six cultivated peach trees, apparently all had poultry and eggs, six produced molasses, seven cut cord wood, and three had built some fencing.

Pennytown resident Dick Green, who had told his children of getting on a wagon in Virginia to help unload it and arriving in Arrow Rock on a boat months later, was "long remembered as an expert sorghum maker." He had produced eighty gallons of molasses, the highest in that category in the 1880 census. Fielding Draffen wrote of his great-grandfather:

> I often tell people that Grandpa Dick was put out of business by the Karo Syrup Company. . . . He made molasses and sold it around the community until syrup became popular in the grocery stores. Although the odds were stacked against him he gave it his best shot and handed down to his children what was most valuable in those days, land.

Through a study of documents and the collection of oral remembrances, Morrow and Kremer learned how the founders of Pennytown had built a stable community through cooperation with their neighbors. Adult women worked in the homes of neighboring white families while older women and those too young to work took care of the children. Men worked for white farmers in exchange for "runt pigs." One would barter for a male, another for a female; they would breed the swine and divide the brood. Each family with swine kept a "hog killing book," and families would gather for hog killings. During the year everyone would gather wood, and in December men would go around with axes and chop the winter's firewood.

Like the Missouri and Osage Indians before them, Pennytown residents became expert "gatherers." "In season they collected large numbers of gooseberries, walnuts, hazelnuts, and hickory nuts." In a nearby woods they found "mushrooms and wild greens—lambs quarter, carpenter's square, wild tomato, lettuce, mustard, poke, and dandelion." Women stored dried fruits in paper bags and stone jars.

Pennytown children attended Thornlea School, and families soon built a Freewill Baptist and a Methodist Church. They had folk remedies and folk medicine practitioners and used a midwife, but a doctor, Tom Hall, delivered many babies in Pennytown homes, "trading his services for Pennytown labor." When the Baptist Church burned in 1924, Pennytown residents raised funds and rebuilt it with tile blocks. Hall donated a parcel of land south of the church that became known as the "Hall Ground." Some of Pennytown's white neighbors helped members of the community, lending them money and renting them land, but others did not welcome the development of the all-black town. At one point, Pennytown residents held a mock "going away" party for Joseph Penny because of threats against him. He sold his property after a few years, but he continued to live in the village with his family.

In 1846, Francis Parkman had noted, "The Missouri is constantly changing its course; wearing away its banks on one side while it forms new ones on the other. Its channel is shifting continually; islands are formed and then washed away; and while old forests on one side are undermined or washed off, a young growth springs up on new soil on the other." In about 1914, after a flood, the river changed course so that it no longer flowed under the Arrow Rock.

By the 1920s, when Ruth and Jake Banks's children were born, the couple lived on the Robert Thompson farm outside Arrow Rock. However, farm technology had improved and less labor-intensive crops were grown; therefore, even fewer workers were needed. Many black families moved to larger towns, where work was easier to find. Others, like Ruth and Jake Banks, moved into Arrow Rock; some bought their own homes. In 1920 the population of Arrow Rock was down to 286; 117 were black.

In the early 1920s, life in Arrow Rock was good for most residents, black and white. Folks worked hard, but they had good times. Dorothy Mosley Kruger was born just outside Arrow Rock. Her grandmother was a Sappington, but she was not a direct descendant of John Sappington. Instead she traces her ancestry on her mother's side to Benjamin Allen Cooper, who first moved to the area in 1808. Kruger remembers her childhood as a happy time:

> In those days we didn't have a lot of things; we were the poorer class, but we didn't know any better. My mother made our clothes out of feed sacks. We raised chickens. We thought we were all right. Mother would make candy . . . especially caramel candy. My sister and I slept in a bedroom and it was cold in there and mother would put the candy in there where it would keep cold. You can imagine what two kids would do. We always sampled the candy. I made that same recipe every year until prevented by health problems. For Christmas my grand dad . . . we called him Big Papa . . . would bring by something like a big delicious apple or an orange. I have no recollection of gifts.

Dorothy recalls the time the Arrow Rock public elementary school for white children burned, and she had an opportunity to meet a resident who was to become as famous in his way as some of the village's earlier settlers:

> Dorothy Craig was a teacher [when] the schoolhouse burned. They always said some boys were smoking and set it on fire. Some children had to go to class on the lower floor of the Masonic Lodge. I went to the Odd Fellows' Lodge. An iron railing on the outside of that building went up to the beautiful meeting room. Jim the Wonder Dog's owner lived right there next door and that's where I got acquainted with him. We children would sit on a rock wall and everybody had to pet him and love him. I was in Marshall one time where Mr. Sam, Jim's owner, ran the hotel. Mr. Sam told Jim to pick out something, a license tag or something about our car, and he came right to our car. He read numbers and letters. He was God's gift to Sam. He had this thing and responded to Mr. Sam. Whether he would have responded to anyone else like that, I don't know.

The schools, though segregated, provided a future for students, both black and white.

Meanwhile, a remarkable lady took steps in the early 1920s that would provide Arrow Rock itself with a future. Nettie Morris Proctor was a pioneer in the effort to preserve the historic village of Arrow Rock.

Nettie's ancestors had fought in the Revolutionary War. One, Robert Morris, signed the Declaration of Independence. She moved to Arrow Rock and soon organized an Arrow Rock chapter of the DAR, then she purchased the Huston Tavern. In 1922 she married Arrow Rock resident L. N. Dickson. His granddaughter, Mary Rinne Stith, described the condition of the tavern at that time:

> The tavern was very run down. Nettie Dickson was very concerned about the structure being saved and being restored and she also felt that there was a tremendous amount of history to be shared. She set up artifacts in the room where today we have the Huston store, and convinced the ladies of the DAR that they could operate the Tavern and serve meals and have lodging and

that with their help, she thought she could convince the state to purchase the Tavern and restore it.

Charles van Ravenswaay, whose family lived in Boonville, grew up with memories of the tavern, where he was taken for Sunday noon-day dinners before the building was rehabilitated. His impression was of "shadowy old rooms, of 'relics' from the early days, and of being in the living past." He wrote, "The small cupola on the roof of the building housing the Tavern bell, and surmounted by a wooden weather vane in the shape of a fish, dates from an early period. A rope connected to the bell extended down into the first floor office and called guests to meals or [rallied] the town residents in the event of fire or other problems." Van Ravenswaay's father, a doctor, got lost on a dark snowy night after seeing a patient in Saline County. "He arrived at the Tavern . . . and finding no one around he rang the bell. Very soon, to his astonishment, the whole town began crowding in to learn what calamity had occurred."

Nettie Dickson managed to save the historic building, and in 1923 the Huston Tavern became the first state-owned facility of Missouri's state park system. Following restoration and remodeling, the historic building was formally opened to the public, with Governor Sam A. Baker delivering an address in May 1926. The accommodations included steam heat and hot and cold water. Meals were served in the dining room.

That same year Missouri established Arrow Rock State Park, stretching over almost thirty-four acres. This included most of the east end of the town, the historic bluff, the town springs, the stone jail, and the white frame academy building, which had been built in the 1850s to house students during the years Joshua L. Tracy was the principal there. Soon, the George Caleb Bingham house also became a part of the park system.

In the summer of 1928, when he was eighteen, Charles van Ravenswaay worked as a clerk in the tavern and had a small antique shop in a nearby building. "The depression throughout the Midwest was a harsh reality; few antique visitors visited Arrow Rock. But my modest sales for the summer seemed a fortune to a teen-ager during those hard times."

Nettie Morris Dickson, who married Arrow Rock resident Lester N. Dickson in 1922, could trace her ancestry back to Roger Williams, pioneer Baptist minister, and Robert Morris, a signer of the Declaration of Independence. She was largely responsible for drawing interest to Arrow Rock as a historic village in the 1920s. (Daughters of the American Revolution, courtesy State Historical Society of Missouri, Columbia)

In the 1930s Athleen Walls was the teacher for the black school. Betty Banks, daughter of Ruth and Jake Banks, was her student from first through eighth grade. Unlike her own mother, Ruth believed her children needed an education. Ruth said, "I thought if they had an 8th grade [education] and they wanted to take up more learnin' later on, they could do that." Black students had to travel to Sedalia for high school. White students went to Marshall, Boonville, or Slater.

In an article published by the *Sedalia Democrat*, Betty Banks Finley tells about growing up in Arrow Rock.

> Where I lived, we had a backyard well to get our water for washing. I remember those days when we washed our dishes in a pan and bathed in a washtub. We had an outhouse, too.
>
> The big spring where we got our drinking water for the family was down in the park. My father always had a wagon and a horse to haul the water.

My mother had a garden she put up for the winter months. I loved my mother's homemade jams, jellies, apple butter and strawberry preserves. Mother did a lot of canning. She also fried down meat and put it in jars. She helped cook at the old tavern. She was a good cook.

One of the most exciting things to happen in Arrow Rock came once or twice a year; It was when a show boat floated to the town. You could hear the music before it got to town. People would be waiting to greet the boat.

Many of the colored people lived in log cabins and made them into a house. I remember using kerosene lamps to see by at night. We burned wood and coal and sometimes kerosene to keep warm. I worked in the potato fields and also chopped down the sorghum cane.

My parents taught me to say "ma'am" and "sir." The town had a grocery store, a drug store, a post office and a bank. There were two doctors in Arrow Rock and a boots and shoe store. There was even a cab run by a white man. Everyone in Arrow Rock made you feel at home. The skin color in this small town did not mean anything.

The town had only three sides, the fourth being the river. I used to love watching the river flow. You could cherish the peace of Arrow Rock.

In March of 1937, the black-and-white setter known as "Jim, the Wonder Dog," who had entertained thousands, died at age twelve. His death was national news. He was buried near Ridge Park Cemetery in Marshall in an area that was later annexed to the cemetery. Jim's owners, Mr. and Mrs. Sam Van Arsdale, had moved about to several area towns, where they operated hotels, and wherever they were, Jim performed for passersby. He performed in the hotel lobbies, at the Chicago World's Fair, and once demonstrated his abilities for a joint session of the state legislature "where he carried out instructions that were written or spoken in Spanish, French, German, and tapped out in Morse code. Many who saw him perform described his ability to find among other 'assignments' a given license number, the animal doctor in the crowd, and the girl in the red and white dress."

Dorothy Mosley Kruger, who had met Jim as a child, recalls living in her grandparents' tenant house during the time that her Grandfather Brockway, a prosperous cattleman and landowner, would go to Arrow Rock to hire forty men at harvest time. "Most of these were blacks, who would be sitting along the street, and he'd pick them up. And it took 40 men to fill a silo. We never did segregate ourselves, but the house where Big Papa lived had two dining rooms—one for the hired help and one for the family. We always had good relations."

The farm economy suffered in the late 1920s and worsened during the '30s. Dorothy's Grandfather Brockway lost all his land and the big house. Coupled with drought, which was especially disastrous for the farming economy, the Great Depression of the 1930s caused considerable hardship in the area. While many farmers and other businessmen in Saline County lost everything, the county rallied and survived.

The increased industry of World War II drew more and more farm laborers to the cities, where they were put to work in plants that built airplanes and manufactured other war supplies. Some families—like Ruth and Jake Banks and their girls, Rachel, who died young, Lucy May, and Betty—stayed in Arrow Rock during the war, working and remaining active in community, school, church, and social affairs as well as service projects. Ruth agreed that they didn't need to make much money because they produced their own food:

> We raised our own hogs to butcher. Butchered our calf. We didn't have to buy that. We had pens we built and hog houses right where we lived. We had a sow and she sometimes had sixteen pigs. We sugar cured the hams and the sarges [sausage] we fried down. We had a [sausage] mill and we'd season it. We raised our own potatoes. Jake buried the potatoes in the winter time and he'd go . . . and get out potatoes for the week. . . . We'd put up beans and cabbages and can tomatoes.

Besides cooking and cleaning for area families, while taking care of her own family, Ruth did volunteer work during the war. She explained, "In the Army time where women was havin' babies and they wasn't able to sew, I made little gowns for the babies and little robes and some white person would bring me the different color blanket goods and I made little serving blankets to wrap the babies in and we sent them across over to them."

Travelers continued to discover the charm of Arrow Rock during the war. In 1944 a family from Arizona visited. A soldier, his wife, and their two-year-old daughter spent his leave time from Ft. Leavenworth in Arrow Rock. Four days' worth of food and lodging cost $24.95.

Mary Rinne Stith, who grew up in the area, recalled that by the late '40s, Arrow Rock was practically a ghost town.

> There were many vacant stores and homes. We had a general store and a locker plant. This was when I was first introduced to a freezer. We dressed chickens and brought them in and stacked them up in the locker. Once a week we'd come to town to get meat out of the locker. In the store there was a vinegar barrel and when it came pickling time, we'd bring in our jug and they'd pump out vinegar into our jug and we'd take it home to make pickles.
>
> I also can remember street dances. They would have a small band come in and play music. Families came to town. Mom and Dad would dance and the children would play. I do remember in the black community there was Whitsey's where they would come and dance and we would beg to come to town to purchase barbecue there and we would take it home to eat. We'd always go in before it got dark and sometimes you'd see a couple dancing. They always had more of a beat to their music. We enjoyed watching their dance and their foot steps.

She also recalled some of the town's special individuals:

> We had a gentleman that lived in Arrow Rock by the name of Mr. Earl Kuhn. His job was to light the lanterns along the river banks so that the barges could see where they were supposed to go. My dad had a saw mill, and he and his workers went across the river and cut logs and one night the boat turned over and when Mr. Kuhn went to light the lights, he found them. One of

the men couldn't swim, and my dad and the other men kept him hanging onto the logs.

Another gentlemen ran a taxi in town; . . . but he came out to the house and got my mom, my sister, and me . . . it was before my brother was born . . . and took us to Arrow Rock. They had all the men in bed and were giving them chicken broth and the doctor had come to check on them and they were going to be all right, but if Mr. Kuhn hadn't come down to light the lanterns, we could have had a catastrophe.

Only a few residents, such as Kruger, Banks, and Stith, stayed in the area and remained actively involved. But many who moved away never quite left for good. They maintained ties with the small town and often returned to reminisce about its past or join in its celebrations. Arrow Rock was home and they loved it still.

Chapter 8

Historic Site
1950–2000

T he village that had witnessed the nation's westward expansion in the 1800s found renewed life in the 1950s. Although its population continued to decline, Arrow Rock again became a place to visit for those interested in national and state history who wanted to experience the sights and sounds of frontier life. As a result of economic conditions that had limited growth, and early efforts by the DAR, the Missouri Department of Natural Resources, and the Friends of Arrow Rock to preserve its heritage, the village had remained pretty much as it was in the 1800s. As Charles van Ravenswaay wrote in 1959, "It remains . . . a museum piece of Missouri's frontier years, expressed in the idiom of the middle south from which most of its early settlers came. There is no town in the state so well preserved, or which expresses so well this particular part of our history."

Van Ravenswaay spoke from experience, having traveled throughout the state two decades earlier to research *Missouri: A Guide to the "Show-Me" State* for the Works Projects Administration (WPA) in the state of Missouri. The National Park Service confirmed his view by designating the tavern and the sites associated with the Santa Fe Trail, including the undeveloped landing and the spring, as National Historic Landmarks in 1963. The George Caleb Bingham house gained this honor later, and the entire village and state park have now been designated a National Historic Landmark by the U.S. National Park Service.

During the late 1950s and 1960s, researchers from the University of Missouri conducted extensive archaeological work at what became known as the "Utz Site" on the Missouri River. Publicity about the findings there brought visitors from across the nation and abroad to Saline County to observe the work and to learn about the Missouri Indians who had lived there two centuries earlier. According to the *Marshall Democrat News* of March 26, 1960, the site became a "research center in archaeology" at the urging of Henry Hamilton of Marshall, president of the Missouri Archaeological Society, and Carl Chapman of the University of Missouri. Chapman reported, "One Sunday last summer . . . 1,691 persons visited the field camp." Further, "a member of the French Embassy from Canada came to Van Meter in the interest of Fort Orleans." Chapman believed that the site of the fort would be discovered if the remains had "not been covered by the river." Most of the area in which fieldwork was done is included in Van Meter State Park.

During the 1950s, the Missouri State Society of the Daughters of the American Revolution continued to operate the tavern. Ruth Banks Perry loved the days she spent as head cook at the tavern. She recalled:

> It was really wonderful. We had a lot of people that would come through goin' to Columbia to the football game. Sometimes we'd have one hundred to cook for. They'd come through at night and stop and have supper. We'd 'pare supper for them . . . fried chicken, ham, green beans, and egg plant . . . escalloped egg plant, and potatoes, light rolls, and sweet rolls. Then they'd order these little tartches [tarts]; sometimes I'd bake one hundred tartches. Or they'd order chocolate pie and sometimes they'd just want cake and ice cream.

The state DAR regent suggested that a Friends of Arrow Rock group be organized. One was formed in 1959, and members interested in preserving Arrow Rock's history recruited supporters from across the nation. Their primary goals were the preservation and restoration of historic structures in the village and the education of visitors. As one of their first projects they purchased the old courthouse, which they restored and donated to the state. About the same time, area residents formed a craft club in order to master and demonstrate skills that pioneers had brought to the frontier, such as making clothing, quilts, soap, and candles. A drama group, sponsored by John Lawrence of Arrow Rock and others, began the Lyceum Theatre in the abandoned Baptist church. Soon seasonal performances began drawing audiences from throughout the state and beyond. The Missouri Department of Natural Resources maintained campgrounds and a picnic area, which attracted numerous visitors.

The year-round population decreased steadily as older residents died and others moved to find work. Jake Banks died and was buried in the section of Sappington Cemetery that John Sappington had given to Banks's ancestor for a black burial ground. Ruth moved to Marshall to find work "when the Tavern slowed down and people wasn't comin' in like they was." She remarried, to a farmer named Perry, and was able to stop working.

In 1969, Jane Froman, the nationally acclaimed singer who had retired to Columbia in 1960, met Arrow Rock resident Jay Turley while they were working with the Easter Seal Society. The two collaborated on developing a music camp in Arrow Rock. Soon a group opened a show at the old schoolhouse, which Turley first called the Arrow Rock Opera House but soon renamed the Jane Froman Music Center. Froman appeared in several programs and concerts in December of 1969. In 1971 Columbia College became involved with the music camps. On June 16, 1972, a special fund-raiser called "Jane Froman Day" was held to finance the new Arrow Rock Arts Series. Local performers and internationally known artists performed in Arrow Rock that summer.

That same summer, the Missouri Tourism Commission announced that a musical version of Mark Twain's *Tom Sawyer* was to be filmed in Arrow Rock. The story was set in a Mississippi River town, resembling Twain's Hannibal, Missouri, as it was in the 1830s or '40s. Arrow Rock had retained enough of the necessary nineteenth-century atmosphere to be chosen as the filming site, though film crews still had to bury electrical lines, cover Main Street with dirt, and construct false building fronts. Several hundred mid-Missourians worked as extras in the film, and many had speaking parts. The Christian

⟲ Jane Froman became interested in Arrow Rock after she retired to Columbia, and the old schoolhouse, built in 1929, was once known as the Jane Froman Music Center. According to Ilene Stone, Froman biographer, "Jane hoped that the center could help young artists achieve their own 'magic moments' through summer music camps and programs." However the music camp and its concerts ended "soon after the 1972 concert series." Froman is shown here with local performers. (Western Historical Manuscript Collection, Columbia)

Church, built in 1872 and owned by the Friends of Arrow Rock, was the scene of the funeral service held for Tom Sawyer, who was missing and presumed dead, while he and Huck Finn hid in the church and listened to the proceedings before they reappeared to a shocked, but pleased, congregation. The next summer the movie company returned to film *Huck Finn,* the story that many consider Twain's masterpiece.

Additional groups formed to support Arrow Rock's efforts to present itself to the public. The Historic Arrow Rock Council (HARC) acquired the old schoolhouse, formerly the Jane Froman Music Center, and renamed it yet again. It became Stolberg Jackson Community Center for "new comer" sisters who had retired to the village. The building is used for events with groups of 150 or fewer, such as the annual Boonslick Music Festival, the Merchants' Antique Show and Sale, and special programs sponsored by the Missouri Arts Council. The Lyceum Theatre used the center for a number of seasons as a rehearsal hall.

In 1981 students from the University of Missouri School of Journalism selected Arrow Rock for an in-depth photographic study to be included in a series of books relating to towns along the Missouri River. Although the river had changed its course decades before, project planners recognized the significance of the village as an early Missouri River town. The result was *Arrow Rock: Twentieth-Century Frontier Town,* a collection of interviews, photographs, and articles that provides a unique insight into the lives of Arrow Rock residents. At that time the town boasted a population of eighty, including eleven children. Pets outnumbered children living in the village. Most of the residents, pets included, posed for a group picture on Main Street.

In 1981 twelve of the thirteen black residents of Arrow Rock still lived on Morgan Street, two streets north of Main Street, although the Arrow Rock School had integrated in 1955 and the last vestiges of segregation had quietly ended in 1968. According to townspeople, until that time African American restaurant customers had to stand or eat outside. The change in racial relations occurred after Martin Luther King's assassination, when a group of young black outsiders came in and sat at a table to eat, "thus beginning integration in Arrow Rock."

By the mid-twentieth century, Pennytown had no residents, but the Freewill Baptist Church was still standing, and it drew former residents and their descendants back for annual reunions, held the first Sunday in August, near Black Emancipation Day, August 4. One former resident, Josephine Lawrence, became a driving force in documenting and preserving the history of the settlement. She

☙ Fielding Draffen, great-great-grandson of Dick Green, a slave before
the Civil War, with his wife, Nancy, Theresa Van Buren Habernal, and
Thelma Conway. Theresa and Thelma were active in the Brown's Chapel
Freewill Baptist Church and well known for their music. Draffen remembers, "When I was a kid, August 4 [Emancipation Day] was sacred to black
people." There are several theories about why August 4 came to be celebrated as Emancipation Day by African Americans; one holds that it was
chosen as a parallel celebration of July 4, "Independence Day." (Friends of
Arrow Rock)

remembered that as a student at Thornlea School, she had failed an assignment to write a history of Pennytown because she could not find any information. The teacher, Frank Brown, had made her stand in a corner on one foot for not having done her assignment.

Much later, her work and that of others led to the selection of the Pennytown Freewill Baptist Church as a National Historic Site in 1986. The church was completely restored in 1998. The results of Lawrence's work are now available to researchers at the Western Historical Manuscript Collection, University of Missouri–Columbia.

A significant boon to the village of Arrow Rock was the completion of the Missouri Historic Site visitor center in 1991. It provides meeting rooms, a library, and exhibit space. Permanent exhibits trace the history of the area and include three original portraits by George Caleb Bingham. Park staff use art or artifacts related to the 1800s to develop displays in the temporary exhibit space.

Mary Rinne Stith, tourist assistant for the Arrow Rock Historic Site, conducts tours, greets visitors, and oversees the younger staff. Mary expressed a feeling common to the volunteers who have worked to preserve and promote their historic town. "To be able to talk to people about my relatives being [among] the first settlers is really exciting."

After the center was built, Mary helped wax the floor, clean, arrange the displays, and demonstrate early crafts, but her involvement with the town began earlier. In fact, the lives of Mary and her family parallel the existence of Arrow Rock. She was born in the area and is descended from Daniel Thornton, one of the first settlers in Cox's Bottom. Family tradition holds that Thornton was the first to plant wheat in the area. He gave the land for Concord Church, where many of Mary's maternal relatives are buried. When Mary was in the eighth grade, her great-grandfather, who was the park superintendent, gave her a steel engraving of George Caleb Bingham's *The County Election,* telling her, "This gentleman in the group of three is Daniel Thornton, and you are a descendent of his." Mary's husband, Bob Stith, a retired schoolteacher, also has roots in the village. His grandfather was town constable and later his father, another park superintendent, taught the Stith children to appreciate their family history, especially as it relates to Arrow Rock history.

☺ The Lyceum Theatre was originally housed in the 1872 Gothic Revival-style Baptist church, the same church that had once scheduled services whenever steamboats docked at Arrow Rock. The theater has expanded, and the church now is the foyer. With support from the Missouri Arts Council and its many loyal patrons, the Lyceum celebrated its forty-fourth season in 2004. (Photo by Samuel R. Davis Jr.)

As part of the Pioneer Life program conducted by the Historic Site, the Friends of Arrow Rock, and volunteers, Mary demonstrates weaving for groups of children, who then tour the John P. Sites Gun Shop and home.

Besides learning about Missouri history, many visitors come to Arrow Rock to enjoy performances at the Lyceum Theatre, which feature professional actors from across the nation. The Lyceum is Missouri's oldest professional regional theater and the only professional theater serving rural Missouri. According to Michael Bollinger, former artistic director, the Lyceum has received two Missouri Arts Awards, its casts have performed at the Smithsonian Institution, and it has established a history of mounting new works. "Annual attendance averages 33,000–35,000 . . . not bad considering Arrow Rock's

☾ The outcome of a *charette,* or brainstorming session, sponsored by the Missouri Humanities Council, was the development of reenactors, such as Loyd French and Carrie Morrow, acting the parts of John Sites and a servant girl welcoming visitors to the Sites Gun Shop during "Gunstocks and Bustles" weekend. (Photo by author)

entire population is less than 100!" Area residents enjoy the performances, but busloads of visitors from Kansas City, St. Louis, Columbia, and even farther away make up the larger part of the enthusiastic audiences.

The Friends of Arrow Rock have an updated office on Arrow Rock's Main Street and oversee tours, education projects, and twelve buildings. One of the buildings, a gift from Bill and Cora Lee Miller, is the home that Charles M. Bradford enlarged in the early 1840s. The house remained in the Bradford family until 1898. Today it houses an antique business. In the late 1990s, Brown Chapel and the Black Lodge Hall, an African American Masonic Lodge from 1881 to 1931, donated by Ted and Virginia Fisher to the Friends of Arrow

Representatives from the University of Tennessee, the Missouri Archaeological Society, and Friends of Arrow Rock sponsored a dig at the Brown Lodge, an African American Masonic building (1881–1950s). The lot was once the site of the Caldwell Pottery Factory (1855–1870s). The lodge has been restored to house an exhibit highlighting the African American history of Arrow Rock. (Photo by author)

Rock, became the site of an ongoing study of African American history. Scholars and students were welcomed to participate as Tim Baumann conducted archeology digs on the site of the two-story building. The Masons had met on the second floor, above a restaurant and tavern on the ground level. Previous digs had investigated the pottery factory, which was once on the property. According to Charles van Ravenswaay, a pottery factory "now in successful operation" was offered for sale in the *Boonville Weekly* in 1855 and remained in operation in 1860.

Sue Hall, Arrow Rock's only black resident in recent years, and Teresa Habernol, who grew up in Arrow Rock, have taken leadership roles in representing the black culture of the area. Their efforts include homecomings for former residents, gospel sings, and Juneteenth celebrations. Since the early 1990s, Arrow Rock, like many other communities across the nation, has held a gathering on a mid-June weekend to commemorate the June 19, 1865, reading of the proclamation that freed Texas slaves. This was two years after President Lincoln's 1863 Emancipation Proclamation, which had freed slaves in states under Confederate control.

Current projects of the Friends of Arrow Rock include updating the Sappington Museum and continuing the restoration of the Lawless farmstead on the edge of town, which began in 2001. Plans include allowing visitors to see the farm in operation. "Also," according to Kathy Borgman, Friends' executive director, "bottom land where the ferry landing and the warehouses were located, plus the Arrow Rock bluff mentioned on maps and in explorers' journals as early as 1732, can be developed."

By the first decades of the twentieth century, as automobile traffic became more common, businesses in Arrow Rock were urging travelers to come through their village. A flyer from the time provided a map across the state, distances from more than thirty towns between Kansas City and St. Louis, and highway directions for travelers going west or east: "Tourists, don't be misled. Follow the Santa Fe Trail. Cross the Missouri River at Arrow Rock. Shortest and best route between Kansas City and St. Louis." Tourists could cross the river at Arrow Rock on the new steamer *Santa Fe,* which could carry seven to ten cars and operated from 7 A.M. to 9 P.M. from June 1 through October 1, and during daylight hours after October 1. Today the shortest route across the state is not through Arrow Rock, but according to guidebooks such as *Country Roads of Missouri,* the route through Arrow Rock to Independence is one of the most historically interesting of Missouri's country roads.

Epilogue

www.arrowrock.org
Arrow Rock Today

For more than two centuries Arrow Rock has touched the lives of hundreds of thousands of people. Some chose to live in the area for a short time or even a lifetime; others simply passed through. People came on foot and by cart or wagon; by canoe, dugout, keelboat, ferry, or steamboat; by car, bus, bike, and motorcycle; and many now visit via the Internet.

Through the years, descendants of early settlers who stayed in the area or returned after a time away have participated in activities that reflect their family histories to those who visit. Gordon Buckner, a retired businessman, was born and grew up in Marshall, Arrow Rock's neighbor and the Saline County seat. His earliest Arrow Rock paternal ancestor, Jay Potter, arrived with his older brothers and mother in the early 1840s after the death of their father. They lived with their mother's brother, H. S. Mills, who ran a store. Jay clerked in the store until his uncle sold it. He then operated a general store and bookstore in Arrow Rock, which advertised medicines, stationery, textbooks, Bibles, hymnals, toys, and school supplies for sale. Buckner remembers many family stories:

> The home of my great grandfather and great grandmother, Jay Marcellus and Wilhelmina Durrett Potter, was located one block east of the Arrow Rock Lyceum. . . . The year of 1865, during the Civil War, my grandmother Daisy Potter was born. Because of the war between the states and other difficulties,

Wilhelmina traveled to the relatively safe state of Iowa to give birth to Daisy. However, being strong states rights advocates, Daisy's place of birth was recorded as Arrow Rock, Missouri, instead of the Northern state of Iowa. Daisy was only six years old when her father died at the relatively young age of 33 years. Her mother then married Will H. Wood and subsequently they moved to Marshall where Daisy later married and became Daisy Potter Buckner.

An event of his childhood that stands out in Buckner's mind was a reunion held east of the Lyceum, just beyond the historic Potter home, in the gazebo that overlooks the river. There his parents and his dad's sisters picnicked where their ancestors had certainly watched the boats on the Missouri River decades before.

Thomas Hall, president of the Friends of Arrow Rock since 2004 and trustee since 1984, a descendant of Matthew Walton Hall, shares an ancestor with Gordon Buckner—Jay Potter. Tom's parents, Dr. and Mrs. Thomas B. Hall Jr., who had a summer home in Arrow Rock from 1966 to 1974, were charter members of the Friends of Arrow Rock, and his father was a trustee of the Friends and chairman of the town board of Arrow Rock. In 1969 Tom earned his degree from Washington University Medical School in St. Louis, which developed from the old Missouri Medical College, where his grandfather Thomas B. Hall Sr. studied medicine.

Dorothy Mosley Kruger, who grew up in the area, married a local widower, Frank Kruger, in 1936. For over sixty years, they have lived on a farm just outside Arrow Rock. Frank had a trucking business, and in addition to raising a family, they have been active in church and community affairs. Dorothy is the only surviving member of the 1959 group that met to organize the Friends of Arrow Rock at the suggestion of the state DAR regent, Mrs. Eads of Columbia. Through the years she helped raise funds for the Friends of Arrow Rock by cooking and serving food during the annual craft festival. Dorothy now sees that the second Sappington cemetery in the area, Sappington Grove Cemetery on Road 129, is tended; her great-grandparents and great-great-grandparents are buried there. Dorothy explains that her involvement in Arrow Rock activities benefits her

☙ Arrow Rock's unique one-man jail inspires speculation about prisoners and provides a place to pose for visitors Carol and Sam Davis. Legends abound about this seldom (if ever) used 1873 addition to the village. Some tell of a man who was incarcerated for drunkenness and made so much noise that the park superintendent let him out so nearby residents could sleep. (Photo by author)

as well as visitors. "Once when I was volunteering in the Friends' office, where I remind folks to sign the register, a lady from the state of California said that one of her ancestors was very active in the area in the 1800s. It turned out to be my ancestor, too . . . Benjamin Cooper."

Donna Klepper Huston has served on the Friends of Arrow Rock board for twenty years. At times she dresses in costume of the 1800s to take schoolchildren on tours of the tavern that Joseph Huston Sr. built. She says that the children love to ring the bell and hear the ghost stories associated with the tavern, which is often still called Huston Tavern.

Donna shares Huston family information with tour groups, telling them that Joseph Huston Jr., as a youth, entered his father's store as clerk and continued there until he came of age, when he entered the grocery business himself and later went into partnership with a good friend, Will H. Wood. This firm conducted a general mercan-

☉ Chuck Holland, like his great-great-grandfather, Henry Wilhelm, active-ly participates in the Arrow Rock tradition of welcoming visitors. (Photo by author)

tile, warehouse, and steamboat business, and was the first firm to sell farm equipment in Saline County. In 1874, Will Wood and Joseph Huston opened the Wood and Huston Bank in Marshall, Missouri. "From the day they moved into Arrow Rock, the Hustons have taken an active part in making Arrow Rock a wonderful village to visit."

Mary Burge's earliest paternal connection to Arrow Rock is Samuel W. McMahan, son of Samuel McMahan, who served under Sarshall Cooper in the War of 1812. Samuel W. was killed by Indians about 1814 when he left the fort to get water. Her Hogge ancestors came to Saline County from Virginia after the Civil War. "They had lost their bank, land, and slaves, so they loaded up what they could in a wagon and came west to farm." In addition to farming, Mary's dad, Albert Hogge, and her Uncle Henry were cattle buyers, in busi-ness as the Hogge Brothers. Their families lived together in a nine-room house called "Magnolia Vale." Each brother had a mule, as did Jess, a black town resident. "Jess came out to the farm early each day, and most times he'd hitch up the mule and take the children to school. While farming, the mules, hitched together, worked as a three-mule team."

While Mary was growing up in the 1930s and 1940s, most of her family's activities were centered around church and school. Special events included DAR activities, community picnics, the Masonic Lodge fish fry, and eating at the tavern. The family attended the Arrow Rock Methodist Church, where before age five Mary sang solos. By the time she attended the University of Missouri in Columbia, each church in Arrow Rock had only about four families, so she was interested when one of her professors mentioned a movement toward the federation of churches. After the professor came to meet with the churches in 1951, the Baptist, Christian, Presbyterian, and Methodist Churches federated. Her future husband and his family were Baptist, so after federation they all went to the same church. The Burges have remained active in the church and in village organizations.

> As a former school teacher, I enjoy helping the Friends and the Site with the school program. We dress like the teachers would have dressed in the 1840s and tell students what life would have been like. I also became Nannie Sites when we started first-person tours. I help the Gospel Sing of old time gospel music. The church is always filled.

Chuck Holland has always felt a kinship to Arrow Rock, but until he purchased the old Hogge place and restored it, he didn't know why. At that time his dad said, "You brought the family back home." Bringing out the Wilhelm albums and family Bible, he showed Chuck that he is a cousin to the Hogge girls, Kitty and Mary. In addition to that, Chuck found that an ancestor, Henry Wilhelm, who came from Kentucky to Arrow Rock in 1836, had suffered a family tragedy soon after his arrival:

> My great great grandfather, Henry St. Joseph Wilhelm, came to Arrow Rock to open a tailor shop. He married Mary Anne Lawless, who was the stepdaughter of Joseph Huston who built the tavern. The couple operated the tavern for awhile. The family Bible indicates that just after their son, John Huston

Wilhelm, was born, while Henry Wilhelm was looking after travelers, his wife, Mary Anne, disappeared, leaving the baby. Wilhelm followed his wife's footprints in the snow to the river's edge.

Wilhelm stayed actively involved in the village even after this tragedy. Besides serving on the town board, he was the postmaster longer than any other man had served—1865 to 1885. He was the town recordkeeper and served on the school board. After the Civil War, Wilhelm started the school for blacks. His former slave was a pupil.

Chuck and his wife bought Magnolia Vale, the Hogge "plantation" house, after it had stood empty for twenty-six years. William Price, who married a Sappington daughter, had built the brick part of the house in 1839. The Hollands, the third owners of the house, renamed it "Airy Hill." In addition to having fur-trading rendezvous on his farm, he is salvaging a log cabin in the area and rebuilding it on his property. Chuck explains his participation in Arrow Rock activities:

> Every other year the town has a Children's Craft Festival. I always set up a tent, which I call a lodge, where I display things a trapper would carry with him—a black powder rifle, a pack, and skins. When the town has an event, I do reenactment for that period. Sometimes I come to town dressed as a mountain man and sometimes as an Indian. Other times I dress as a fur trapper. I am part of the local color.

Chuck was a movie extra in both *Tom Sawyer* and *Huck Finn*. In *Huck Finn* he was part of the "Hannibal 13." He remembers: "I was one of the guys who chased the con men."

Dorothy Piper LaRue is a lifelong resident of Saline County. She traces her ancestry to Thomas McMahan and David Jones, who came to the Boonslick area in 1810, and to the Pipers, the Benjamin Hustons, and the Marshalls, who followed when Arrow Rock was still just a place to cross the Missouri River. Although Dorothy and her husband shared the McMahan line, his roots also went back to Peyton Nowlin, Bernis Brown, and Saunders A. Ward Townsend. After her husband's death, Dorothy continued his work with the

☉ Henry Wilhelm, tailor, postmaster, and town board chairman, arrived in Arrow Rock in 1836. After the Civil War he arranged schooling for African American children. (Friends of Arrow Rock)

Townsend Cemetery, and she has researched the early days of settlement in the area:

> The McMahans and Jones built a fort with the Andersons about the time that the British were stirring up the Indians which led to the War of 1812. Benjamin Howard, the territorial governor, sent word to these settlers that they needed to move back east because he couldn't protect them. They refused, but did eventually have to move to other forts until the war was over. They lost men and property, but they did come through. Later, David Jones was appointed to represent this area in the Missouri Territory Legislature and was serving when Missouri applied to become a state.

Dorothy's daughter Jeanne belongs to the weaving guild, which demonstrates at the annual craft festival. They are involved with the annual pig roast in Arrow Rock, which supports the Arrow Rock

Volunteer Fire Department. Dorothy and Jeanne always donate pies—custard, coconut, or gooseberry—and serve them.

Harold Bingham Turley was a descendant of early Arrow Rock settlers John Bingham and Steven Turley. His great-grandfather, John Bingham, uncle of George Caleb Bingham, bought a section of land in 1824 and two more sections in 1826. He and Burton Lawless gave land to begin the town of Arrow Rock. Early Turley settlers, Talson and his son Jesse B., were scouts for Kit Carson. They made several trips to Taos, New Mexico, on the Santa Fe Trail and went to California during the gold rush.

Harold Bingham Turley was born on the farm near Arrow Rock in 1913. He met his wife, Mary Ann, while both were working for the contractors who were building Fort Leonard Wood. Later when Mary Ann came to Arrow Rock to visit Harold and the family, she stayed at the tavern when Flora Page was hostess. After the Turleys married, they returned to the farm in Saline County. Only one other farm in the state has been owned and operated longer by one family.

Mary Ann belonged to the Mary Fisher theater group, which met in Marshall but performed at the Lyceum in Arrow Rock. She recalled the early days of the Lyceum: "The Lyceum was started as a learning thing. The first actors were all drama students who stayed with families in town. The students did everything . . . built sets and acted. You'd see one with a hammer in one hand and his script in the other." For the yearly Hanging of the Greens, Mary Ann dresses as Mrs. Santa. "It takes a lot of people to do all the projects in this town. We've had talented leaders and each project has its own group and everybody seems to like to do what is suggested. Arrow Rock is a community of togetherness."

Mary Lou Pearson's connection with Arrow Rock goes back only to 1937, but she has been interested in Saline County history since then.

> My Aunt Flora Page was hostess of the tavern for the DAR in 1937 when I was still in high school. She used us kids—her son, my sister, and me—as guides through the tavern. She taught me what I know about Arrow Rock. In the five years she was hostess, we kids did the foot work and my aunt did the writing to catalog the records of the Saline County cemeteries. That was fun and

she got us interested in Arrow Rock, of course.

One time I won't forget was when a famous singer was in town to visit the Sappington house. . .she [said she] was related to the Sappingtons. She asked me to park her car in George Pearson's garage next to the tavern. On her keys was her name: Jane Froman.

Mary Lou also recalled when she became the hostess at the tavern.

I was left with two little kids and had to work. The children, Buzzy and Jackie, walked to the Arrow Rock Grade School. The tavern had run down during the war and I worked hard to build it back. Governor Smith was very interested in Arrow Rock. He loved to come over here. He'd call to have us cook breakfast for the House on their way to visit the State School in Marshall or to have dinner for the Senate on their way back.

During the time Mary Lou operated the tavern, she married Arrow Rock native Morris Pearson. Morris's great-grandfather was German immigrant Louis Eversmann, who died before he could move to the farm he had bought in Saline County. Morris's mother was a charter member of the Arrow Rock DAR, which was instrumental in all of the early restorations. His grandfather O. B. Pearson and other Arrow Rock people are in Bingham's paintings, *Stump Speaking* and *The County Election,* so he, too, was interested in and concerned over the future of the village. Mary Lou echoed the feelings of twenty-first-century residents who have ties to early settlers of this village, "Arrow Rock is home."

The late Arvel Townsend always said that according to Saline County history, he was related to early Arrow Rock settlers, but it was obvious his interests lay more in the everyday activities of the village where he had lived nearly all of his life. He left only once, for four years, when he served with the 721st Railway Operating Battalion in India. One day in India, Arvel saw a boy between nine and twelve, just "skin and bones," between the rail and the platform. He picked him up and began sharing his C-rations. He called the boy Dajul, and when he got well, Dajul went with him everywhere. "Dajul learned to speak English and taught me how to speak some Hindu."

Longtime resident Arvel Townsend used to entertain checker-playing visitors on Arrow Rock's Main Street. (Friends of Arrow Rock)

After his army days and retirement from the M-K-T Railroad, Arvel became part of Arrow Rock's "local color": he often sat on the boardwalk playing checkers with passersby. He related, "I hear a lot of different languages sitting on the boardwalk. One day while I was playing checkers here in Arrow Rock, some women were discussing in Hindu where the visitor center was located. I stumbled through the Hindu language to tell them. They were really surprised. People come from all over to come to Arrow Rock."

Today 200,000 visitors a year come—to act in Lyceum productions or see a performance, to view the dig site or to participate in the discovery of the past, to research genealogy or learn history, or to stroll down Main Street or celebrate a special occasion with dinner. Visitors may step back in time and become, for a few hours, part of history in a place that has been, for hundreds of years, on the itinerary of world travelers.

For More Reading

Along the Old Trail: Pioneer Sketches of Arrow Rock and Vicinity, by T. C. Rainey (Marshall, Missouri; Marshall Chapter DAR, 1914), includes remembrances of early settlers in the Arrow Rock area.

Arrow Rock: Crossroads of the Missouri Frontier, by Michael Dickey (Arrow Rock: Friends of Arrow Rock, 2004), is a well-researched and documented history of Arrow Rock, focusing on its origins and development through the Civil War era.

Arrow Rock Places, by Virginia Lee Fisher (Historic Arrow Rock Council, 1988), provides information on early days in Arrow Rock.

Arrow Rock: The Story of a Town, Its People, and Its Tavern, by Charles van Ravenswaay (Daughters of the American Revolution; reprinted from the *Missouri Historical Society Bulletin,* Apr. 1959), includes historical and firsthand accounts of early residents and photos to bring Arrow Rock history to life for the reader.

Arrow Rock, 20th Century Frontier Town, edited by Marcia Joy Prouse (Columbia: University of Missouri School of Journalism, 1981), captures in photographs and accounts the lives of black and white Arrow Rock residents in the 1980s.

Arrow Rock: Where Wheels Started West, by Jean Tyree Hamilton (Friends of Arrow Rock, Inc. 1963), relates the history of early years of the village and includes photographs.

Dictionary of Missouri Biography, edited by Lawrence O. Christensen, William E. Foley, Gary R. Kremer, and Kenneth H. Winn (Columbia: University of Missouri Press, 1999), includes information on many residents of the Boonslick and some who passed by.

First Ladies of Missouri, revised edition, by Jerena East Giffin (Jefferson City: Giffin Enterprises, 1996), introduces in delightful detail the wives of Missouri's governors. The bibliography encourages further reading.

George Caleb Bingham: Missouri's Famed Artist and Forgotten Politician, by Paul C. Nagel (Columbia: University of Missouri Press, 2005), is a study of the two defining aspects of Bingham's life—his career as an artist and his political achievements.

Lewis and Clark in Missouri, 3rd edition, by Ann Rogers (Columbia: University of Missouri Press, 2002), is a well-researched account of the experiences of Lewis and Clark in Missouri.

Nathan Boone and the American Frontier, by R. Douglas Hurt (Columbia: University of Missouri Press, 1998), explores the Boone family's true-life adventures in the Boonslick area and beyond.

The Osage: An Ethnohistorical Study of Hegemony on the Prairie-Plains, by Willard H. Rollings (Columbia: University of Missouri Press, 1992), discusses the impact of European exploration and settlement on the tribe.

The Osage in Missouri, by Kristie C. Wolferman (Columbia: University of Missouri Press, 1997), provides a history of this important tribe in early Missouri.

Resources for More Information

Arrow Rock is thirteen miles north of I-70 on Hwy 41 in Saline County.

Friends of Arrow Rock
P.O. Box 124
Arrow Rock, Missouri 65320
660-837-3231
office@friendsar.org
website: *www.friendsar.org*

Arrow Rock State Historic Site Visitor Center
P.O. Box 1
Arrow Rock, Missouri 65320
660-837-3330
www.dnr.state.mo.us

Arrow Rock Lyceum Theatre
High Street
Arrow Rock, Missouri 65320
660-837-3311
www.lyceumtheatre.org

Historic Arrow Rock Council
P.O. Box 121B
Arrow Rock, Missouri 65320
660-837-3398

Arrow Rock Area Merchants Association
P.O. Box 147B
Arrow Rock, Missouri 65320
660-837-3268

Index

About the Author

Photo by Olan Mills

Authorene Wilson Phillips is a retired secondary English/speech teacher who lives in Marshall, Missouri.